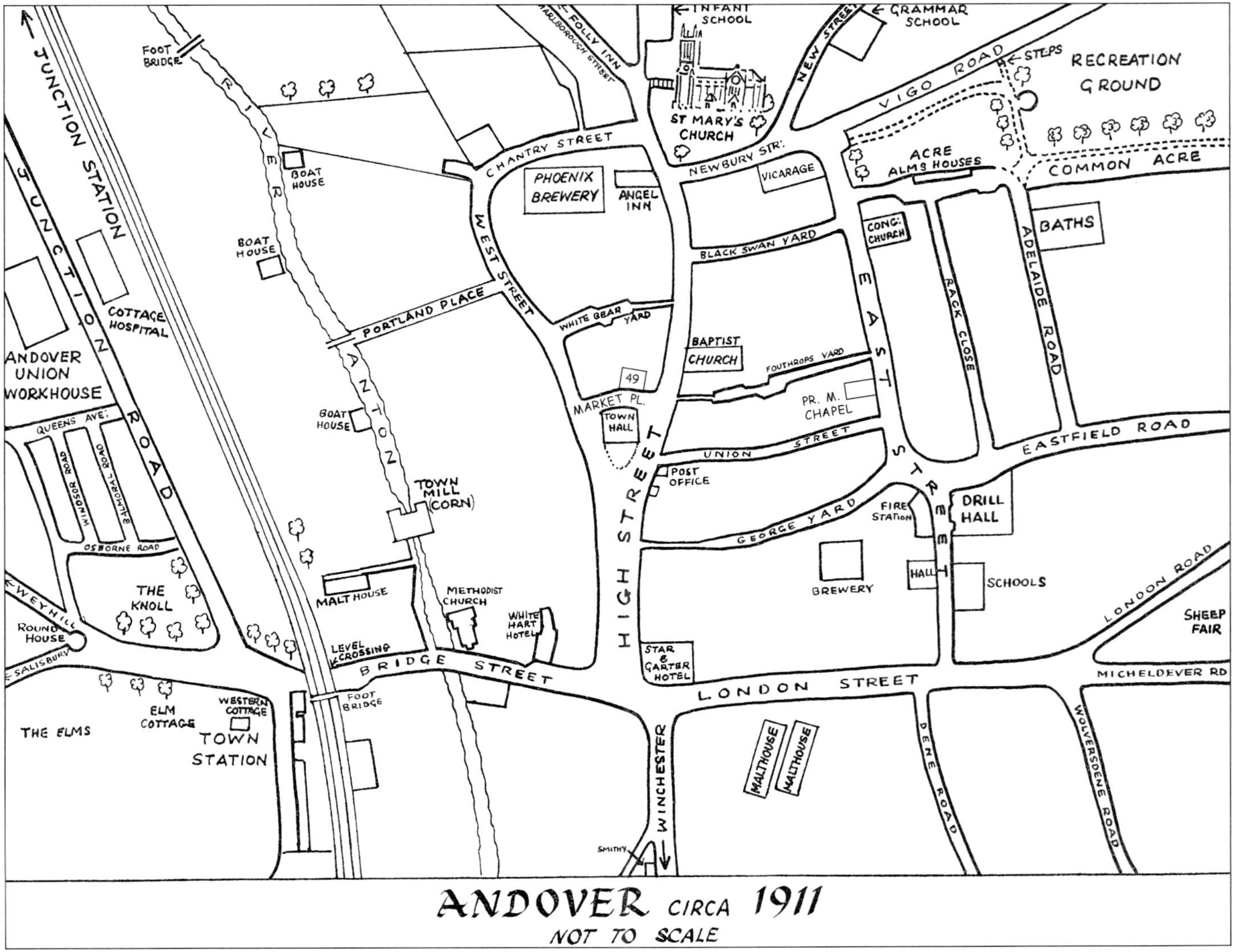

From C.J.J. Berry, *Old Andover* (1976)

AN ANDOVER MISCELLANY

contributed by

DAVID J. BORRETT ANDREW JACKSON

HARRY W. PARIS

Primitive Methodism in Andover

Layton's of Andover

Andover Cottage Hospital

Andover in the Great War 1914-1918

Index of 19th century Andoverians

ANDOVER HISTORY & ARCHAEOLOGY SOCIETY

2008

AN ANDOVER MISCELLANY

Published by Andover History and Archaeology Society
c/o Andover Public Library
Chantry Way, Andover SP10 1LT.

ISBN: 978-0-903755-23-8

CONTENTS

ILLUSTRATIONS

INTRODUCTION

As its title indicates, this book brings together work by three of Andover's local historians. Each of their contributions was too long for inclusion in *Lookback at Andover,* the annual journal of the Andover History and Archaeology Society, but not really long enough to be published as monographs. A miscellany seemed to be the answer.

David Borrett, who edits *Lookback at Andover*, has contributed two major articles. His 'Layton's of Andover. The History of a China and Glass Warehouse 1853-1952' recounts the fortunes of one of the town's longest trading shops. The society was delighted when Mr Borrett was awarded the Margaret Kyrle Prize for Local History for this work in 2004. His other article is a study of 'Primitive Methodism and the Birth of the Andover Circuit' which adds much to our knowledge of nonconformity in the town and some of the people who became members of the Andover Circuit.

Andrew Jackson has been extracting interesting material about the town from back copies of the *Andover Advertiser* and other sources for some years. We are very pleased that he has been able to put together the story of Andover's Cottage Hospital, which was the predecessor of our War Memorial Hospital. Being methodical in all his research, as he went along he made a note of the names and occupations of many 19th century Andoverians, although he modestly points out that 'This was not a systematic trawl, rather a jotting down of anything I happened to see on my reading travels'. Nevertheless, his splendid list of some 450 names will delight family historians in particular. However, they should be aware that as the list is alphabetical, those names have not been included in the composite index to the four articles.

Sadly, our other author is no longer with us. Harry Paris (1907-2001) touched life in Andover at many points during his long life. In his retirement he made a great contribution to recording the local history of the town, especially of New Street where he had lived as a boy. When writing or preparing talks to the society, he would draw on both his own memories and the files of the *Andover Advertiser.* Several of us remember his vivid description of seeing the wounded arriving at Andover Junction Station in 1916; in his written account he mentions that this was seen by 'two boys' but of course he was one of them. In 1994 the society produced two dozen typescript copies of his patriotic account of 'Andover and New Street in the Great War, 1914-1918' for its members. We are now very pleased to be able to publish this in a more permanent form with the agreement of his son, Mr. Lionel Paris.

It has been difficult to decide in which order the four main studies should appear. Although Harry Paris's account of the town in World War I is the longest and best illustrated, it seemed right to maintain the society's usual practice of proceeding in approximate date order of the different subjects. Thus the articles on Primitive

Methodism and the story of Layton's of Andover come before the two which both finish with accounts of the establishment of the War Memorial Hospital. Footnotes appear at the end of each piece.

As ever, all our historians have been grateful for the facilities and willing help that have always been available at the Hampshire Record Office. This has included the provision of a number of images in digital form from the Hampshire Photographic Project; all those we have used were taken from photographs collected by Harry Paris. It was a great relief to the society when the HRO took the back files of the *Andover Advertiser* into their keeping after the demise of Holmes & Son who had published it from 1876–1986. Reports from its pages are quoted in all the studies. The society is also grateful to the staff of Andover Museum for help on many fronts, including their care of the boxes of Harry Paris's photographs.

Diana Coldicott
editor.

PRIMITIVE METHODISM
AND THE BIRTH OF THE ANDOVER CIRCUIT

David J. Borrett

The religious movement known as Primitive Methodism first began in the area around Mow Cop on the Staffordshire and Cheshire border. Hugh Bourne (1772-1852), a local Methodist, became dissatisfied with the lack of religious energy being generated by the Church in his district and established a system of conversation preaching – the speaking of man to man on spiritual concerns – in his own village of Harriseahead. Soon, as the religious revival gained more and more enthusiasts, the holding of regular cottage-prayer gatherings was developed. In due course a chapel was built, largely at Bourne's expense, in part of the garden belonging to his cousin, Daniel Shubotham. Religious classes were formed and though the independent nature of the situation was irregular, there was as yet no breach with the local Methodist Circuit, for the new chapel received a supply of preachers from the Methodist Circuit authorities who were based at Burslem.

Further religious revivals occurred in the area, such as that started in 1805 by the Tunstall potter, William Clowes, just a few miles south of Harriseahead. In that same year, the American evangelist, Lorenzo Dow, visited the district in order to preach extensively and to publicise the American system of large open-air meetings. Dow's effect was pivotal in that he inspired Hugh Bourne, William Clowes and others to hold the first British camp or open-air meeting on the hillside of Mow Cop on 31st May 1807, an occasion when it was said that several thousand people were converted. It was not long before alarm began to spread among the Burslem Circuit authorities who felt that their own influence was being usurped by this very spontaneous, un-Methodist style movement and they issued pamphlets against camp meetings. Bourne still considered himself a thorough Methodist but refused to back down. Ignoring the wishes of the local circuit masters, he and his supporters organised successive camp meetings to take place in July and August 1807.

In the meantime, the 1807 Methodist conference in Liverpool declared camp meetings to be unconstitutional. The effect of this decision meant far more than just a dispute over internal procedure within the Connexion; because the Conventicle Act of 1664 actually prevented nonconformist clergymen forming congregations of their own, the withdrawal of any official sanction meant that camp meeting preachers were effectively unlicensed and many now declined to proceed further for fear of legal reprisals.

But Hugh Bourne was determined to press ahead and the August camp meeting at Norton-in-the-Moors took place as planned. Retaliation from the official Methodists at nearby Burslem was not long in coming and the Methodist Quarterly Meeting of June 1808 expelled Bourne from the Movement. William Clowes, whose similar Tunstall enterprise was independent of Bourne's, was likewise expelled in June 1810.

After Bourne's expulsion he and his followers became known as the Camp Meeting Methodists but as yet its leader was still hopeful of reuniting the splinter group with the main body. However, the opposition to camp meetings by the mainstream

Methodists was uncompromising and eventually, after much soul-searching on the part of Bourne, a new group was formed which brought together the two rebel factions – the Camp Meeting Methodists and the so-called Clowesites, the followers of William Clowes. By a meeting of February 1812, the name Primitive Methodists was adopted. The term is taken from the final address given by John Wesley in 1790 when he said:

> Fellow labourers, wherever there is an open door, enter in and preach the gospel; if it be two or three, under a hedge or a tree, preach the gospel; go out quickly into the streets and lanes of the city, and bring in the poor and the maimed and halt and blind...this is the way the *primitive Methodists* did.[1]

In due course, rules were drawn up whereby Bourne became General Superintendent and a Tract Society was instituted, as were Sunday schools. The new denomination spread slowly at first, but by 1822 forty-two congregations in the five counties of Staffordshire, Derbyshire, Lincolnshire, Leicestershire and Nottinghamshire had been established. Preachers were itinerant and travelled on foot or on horseback many hundreds of miles to effect their missions of mass conversions. These missionaries often irreparably damaged their health in the process and many died prematurely as a result of their labours. There was no formal training and anyone with sufficient enthusiasm could become a preacher. Bourne encouraged self-education by means of his own works and the connexional magazine. An aspect of the Primitive Methodists from the very beginning was that many of these preachers were women: one such was Sarah Kirkland whose efforts were rewarded by the Connexion spreading to Nottingham in 1817. There was a period of crisis between 1825 and 1828 when it was found that many of the infant local societies had little knowledge of church affairs and suffered because of unsuitable persons acting as ministers. Expulsions followed, new regulations instituted and the Movement revived.

From the early beginnings in Staffordshire, the Connexion progressed southwards into East Anglia, Essex and Huntingdonshire. Soon it would spread further still, but it would be wrong to suppose that preachers had merely to enter a town or village and preach the gospel to the inhabitants for there to be mass conversions and the quick establishment of a Primitive Methodist society. There was often great local opposition, and when attempts were made to extend the Movement into the agricultural southern counties where poverty was rife, that opposition could become extremely virulent. Far from being welcomed as liberators, as perhaps had often been the experience farther north, many of the evangelical 'crusaders' were treated as an invading force and were savagely persecuted. The attempt to bring the Movement into Wiltshire, Berkshire and Hampshire coincided precisely with the period of revolt which gave rise to the spate of rick-burning and machine breaking, just when the mythical "Captain Swing" was wreaking his worst havoc.[2] Ordinary labourers, frightened that their jobs and already subsistence levels of wages would be wiped out by the advent of mechanisation, were taking matters into their own hands and rebelling against the local establishment. Indeed, *ad hoc* groups and seditious factions were urging them to riot in the most public way.

It was into the immediate aftermath of this near-revolution that Thomas Russell, the Primitive Methodist pioneer, rode into Hampshire in late 1830 with his companion John Wride. Russell had already suffered imprisonment for preaching at Chaddleworth in Berkshire but he seems to have possessed great determination. He visited Coombe, then in Hampshire, at the end of 1830, Faccombe in January of the following year, and then Linkenholt, where he noted that Michael Osmond gave him a shilling and thirty others joined him in prayer.[3] Although advised by his Circuit not to go farther until those places already evangelised could be consolidated, Russell decided to go on, at his own risk and expense. By April 1831 he was in Hurstbourne Tarrant, moving from there along the Bourne Valley and on to Stoke and Binley (where, he wrote, Miss Farr and her parents were converted, as were scores of others in their house) and through to St. Mary Bourne.[4] All these villages became part of the recently-formed Shefford Circuit which had itself arisen out of the Brinkworth Circuit.

Despite the receipt of those few crumbs of comfort that Russell cited in his brief memoirs, he must have suffered greatly. Apart from the obvious discomfort of travelling constantly on horseback and the uncertainty of being able to obtain food and lodgings, there were always people only too willing to demonstrate and inflict opposition to his endeavours: 'No ranters here!' and 'Church and King!'[5] are jeers often quoted by commentators, but no doubt there was also much verbal and physical abuse during his journeying. Religion was a deeply serious business in those days and in places where the way of life had not changed for generations, people were fearful for the eventual repose of their souls. It was no wonder that those such as Thomas Russell, preaching in a manner that might seem foreign and unfamiliar, were treated with suspicion, contempt and hostility by the small tightly-knit communities into which they came. We should consider also, especially in the larger communities where the mix of inhabitants cut right across the range of class and social barriers, that there were sizable factions of people whose 'faith' and moral codes were contemptuous of any religion, and were based primarily on the raw instinct necessary for survival; little sympathy was likely to be found here for evangelists such as Thomas Russell.

But despite coming so near, it was not Thomas Russell who brought Primitive Methodism into Andover. Russell's route of 1830-1 would have taken him very close, but it seems whereas he might easily evangelise the smaller villages to the north, crossing the boundaries of a town containing 5000 inhabitants was something quite different. We know that the Circuit authorities were anxious that the Connexion should not spread too far too quickly in case it could not be adequately consolidated; Andover itself may have seemed just too much to take on at that time.

Indeed, perhaps with some justification owing to its recent history of social unrest, Andover might have been thought simply too awful to contemplate. But interestingly, the local incident known as the 'Tasker Riots', when an attack was made on the iron foundry at Anna Valley, well illustrates the potency of religious belief even within the ranks of a rebellious mob: the assault on the works took place on a Saturday, and on the stroke of midnight all the rioters abandoned their frenzy of destruction to go home so as to observe the Sabbath. They returned on the Monday but a detachment of the 9th Lancers had been drafted in and was ready waiting for them. Sixteen men were arrested and tried at Winchester a month later, when eleven were sentenced to be transported for life.[6]

The violence soon petered out but the rumblings of discontent and instability may have lingered about the area for some time afterwards – certainly little had altered to remedy the grievances that had precipitated the uprising in the first place. Whether the troubles were a factor or not, Thomas Russell's successes in the Bourne Valley during early 1831 were not followed up by an attempt on Andover itself, and for the moment the religious surge towards the town came to a halt.

Not until March 1833 did the Quarterly Meeting of the Shefford Circuit decide that George Wallis and William Wiltshire should conduct a missionary enterprise into Andover. A few weeks later, on 5th May, the two preachers, together with various supporters from the Bourne Valley, entered the town.[7] The custom on such occasions was to begin an enthusiastic singing of the rousing religious ballads calculated to gather people into the throng. American-inspired, this music owed much to the influence of Lorenzo Dow. What was on offer here was drama, excitement and fellowship - sharp contrasts indeed for communities beset by poverty and accustomed only to repetitive routines of drudgery.[8] This was something quite new.

As George Wallis and his associates made their way through the town, almost certainly up New Street which was then densely populated, they did indeed draw many people along with them, and with high hopes on the part of the evangelists a religious service was begun, either within the grounds of the Walled Meadow [9] or in the market place.[10] But it was not long before trouble began. Newcomers are often regarded with suspicion, not least when bringing with them an unconventional style of religion, and among the gathered crowd were a few onlookers who took it on themselves to disrupt the proceedings by creating commotion, even trying to knock down the preacher himself. Wallis continued with his service as best he could and persevered to the end. Undaunted, he returned on successive Sundays to repeat the exercise, but instead of gradually winning over more and more of his audience, the demonstrations of opposition became even greater. One particular Sunday was notable for its extreme virulence: with a bawling mob screaming abuse, rushing at him and crying out that he should be put to death, Wallis continued to preach on. With dirt and eggs being hurled from all directions, the crowd continued to jeer, push and attack. Finally, the Constable and the Town Beadle, whose sentiments may well have been more in sympathy with the crowd than its intended victim, reluctantly felt that they should do their duty and attempt to restore order. The official gentlemen made their way through the crowd, grabbed George Wallis by the collar and escorted him away.[11]

The attentions of the mob were not so easily diverted and a loud, vengeful procession, armed with sticks and besoms followed them, taking every opportunity to strike at the preacher, tear the skirts of his coat and subject him to continued abuse. Eventually, he found sanctuary in the house of a sympathiser and the crowd, once deprived of their primary target, turned on Wallis's supporters from the villages of the Bourne Valley and drove them from the town.[12]

History is silent as to what happened next but a resolute determination on the part of the missionaries seems to have eventually paid dividends and a fledgling Andover Primitive Methodist Society came into being. Although this began under the Shefford Circuit, by 1837 the Andover branch had become geographically central to over twenty village branches around it and it was decided to form a new Andover Circuit. Quarterly accounts begin in June 1837.[13] At this point the strength of membership in Andover itself was only 14. In some of the villages assigned to the Andover Circuit it was much greater: Hurstbourne Tarrant had 26 while Collingbourne had 39, though these two northerly branches had been established earlier.[14] And not all those who attended chapel were paid-up members of the connexion; many came as 'hearers' who had no wish to graduate to full membership.[15] Even by the time of the Religious Census of 1851, though the Andover branch had 50 members, its evening service was attended by 120 people who were described as being general congregation and 30 Sunday scholars. Even this was considerably lower than the estimated average evening attendance throughout the year of 230 general congregation and 70 Sunday scholars.[16] Such a figure seems wildly optimistic; it may have been too much of a temptation to exaggerate the figure for purposes of propaganda. An added note records that both general congregation and Sunday scholars varied considerably over twelve months.

Until 1838 there were no purpose-built chapels owned by the Andover Circuit, neither in the town itself, nor in any of the surrounding villages. But it is evident that a building within the town was rented before that – at least for a year or so. The earliest accounts include a quarterly payment of £2 for chapel rent which continues until the opening of the first chapel in East Street, Andover on 21st October 1838.[17] Just a few months earlier, at the June 1838 Quarterly Meeting at Leckford (these meetings were held at varying places in the Circuit) it had been decided 'that we sanction the buying of the premises at Andover for building a chapel', suggesting that the freehold of the rented building was available for purchase and that this was the site envisaged for the new building.[18] Very often the earliest meeting houses of newly-constituted branches were no more than a wooden shed or barn, but it is likely that as this was situated in one of the principle streets of the town the predecessor of the new chapel was a brick-built construction. It may not however, have been ideally suited for their purposes as it stood, or perhaps it was run down; in either case, certainly the Primitive Methodists wasted no time in demolishing it.

A view of East Street, before 1906.

The East Street Primitive Methodist Chapel shortly before its demise, 1967. (HPP34/120)

The Register of Baptisms begins in 1834.[19] This date is surprising. One would expect the baptisms register to run, as the accounts do, from the formation of the new Circuit in June 1837. To add to the confusion, an inscription in the flyleaf reads '19th December 1835'. Perhaps local baptisms were recorded and written up later when the official register arrived. The first entry is on 29th November 1834 and is the entry for nine-day-old Harry Hall, son of the Andover shoemaker, James Hall, and his wife Elizabeth, formerly Keel. These earliest baptisms were not performed by George Wallis but by the travelling preacher, Henry Heyes. It is interesting that although the first entry is an Andover one, there are sixteen others before June 1837, and all except one are for children baptised in the surrounding villages. These ceremonies were probably performed in the homes of the parents, or maybe, reflecting the camp meeting tradition they took place in the open air,[20] – although baptisms in winter to newly-born babies would hardly seem a good idea! That first local baptism in Andover was probably a cause for some celebration by connexion enthusiasts, an event that symbolised the consolidation of Primitive Methodism in the town. It took place on a Saturday so it appears that such occasions were not necessarily part of Sunday worship. Obviously, if a preacher were travelling on foot within a radius of twenty miles or so, baptisms had to be performed when it was practical to do so and, indeed, it does seem that the recording of the subsequent ceremonies in the official register was not always immediate, as several entries are seriously out of chronological sequence.[21]

Between 1833 and 1837, the Andover mission almost certainly had little in the way of finance. Though some degree of funding might come from the parent Circuit, any money which the branches raised was expected to be handed over in order to pay the various Circuit expenses such as the salaries of the travelling preachers or the mortgage debt on the chapels. Where there was not enough money, the preachers were the first to suffer from reduced wages. Once the Andover Circuit had been established, money came in from all the allied branches and the initial income for the quarter ending in June 1837 was £22/13/10d, of which 7/6d was a donation by William Tasker of Waterloo Ironworks. This left a surplus of 7/10d.[22]

Initially, a place to meet in Andover itself may have been provided free of charge: Thomas Russell cited as a measure of his success in the Bourne Valley how scores of people were converted in the house belonging to Miss Farr and her parents. This use of a private house was normal practice in the absence of a chapel, and individuals, enthused with the worthiness of a cause, might willingly lend a room for the regular conduct of Sunday services and those attending these regular gatherings each contributed a small amount of money. Once there was sufficient membership in a particular geographical area – ideally a central nucleus with many closely connecting branches – a new Circuit could be established by means of secession. In this way the countrywide network of Circuits grew ever larger.

Membership of the Connexion was open to all, although strict procedures had to be observed. After professing faith in Jesus Christ and showing consistent evidence of that faith in everyday affairs, prospective members had to be approved by the Quarterly meeting of the Circuit Committee. This could only follow at least three months attendance at the regular religious classes.[23] The Quarterly Meetings book makes note of the membership numbers, and an entry for September 1840 shows that in the Andover branch there were twenty full members, four others were on trial and two further were doubtful.[24] One wonders whether the latter verdict was in the opinion of the Committee or an admission by the individuals themselves? Even after approval, a ticket of membership was renewable quarterly, and if at any time a particular member's conduct was not thought appropriate to his position, he could be expelled. Contributions were expected weekly, as well as a voluntary offering every three months at the issue of tickets.[25]

Maybe it is not surprising that the stringency of membership tended to result in village societies securing greater numbers than Andover itself. In a town there were many secular and non-secular activities in which the inhabitants could interest themselves, whereas in the villages there was likely to be little more than the parish church and the local inn. In this latter situation, where everybody knew everybody else and interests and concerns were rather similar, the establishment of a Primitive Methodist society by some of the villagers could soon draw in many others.[26]

Of all the nonconformist sects, Primitive Methodism was the humblest and the cheapest. There was real endeavour to include the smallest outlying villages and to bring the poorest people into its fold.[27] In the first twenty years of local baptisms (1834-54), during which are recorded about 500 entries, the number of fathers who are stated to be labourers outnumber those of a named occupation by more than 4-1.[28] This is in sharp contrast to those of the Independent or Congregational church whose place of worship lay also in East Street, within a stone's throw of the Primitive Methodist chapel. Here, the membership register reads almost like a roll call of the High Street traders; no doubt class distinctions divided the nonconformist memberships no less than in other walks of life.[29]

The readiness with which all nonconformists of whatever persuasion accepted strict codes of conduct and endorsed wholeheartedly ever-increasing privations to their everyday freedoms and pleasures seems to echo some of those same instincts that inspired the Puritan movement in the seventeenth century. Indeed, the early Congregationalists, the Presbyterians and the Calvinists can all be linked to Puritan thought, and many others of the non-Anglican sects possess similar doctrinal characteristics.[30] For the religious revivalists in the nineteenth century, particularly the Primitive Methodists, the issue of Temperance was a great rallying cry and at the heart of policy from the 1830s onwards.[31] Although the purpose of the national Temperance Movement was for moderation in the consumption of alcohol, rather than total abstinence, inevitably it soon became dominated by more obsessive elements who strove for the more extreme ideal. Temperance was almost like a religion in itself and permeated all levels of society, a mass reaction to the scourge of drunkenness which was seen as a curse on society.[32] These instincts suited the character of Primitive Methodism like no other and church members who abstained completely wore a strip of blue ribbon pinned to their clothing to show that they had 'signed the pledge'. Nobody holding a licence for the sale of alcohol could be admitted to the Primitive Methodist Church and members were often expelled for over-indulgence.[33]

Expulsion was a weapon that was frequently employed. Such was the zealousness of the national Connexion leaders that reports had to be prepared by each Circuit annually in which the names of those who had left the Church during the previous year were listed and a reason given for their departure. The 1848 report of the Andover Circuit tells us that 'John Mansfield' had 'fallen by drunkenness', 'Charlotte Soper fell from grace' (a euphemism for prostitution or pregnancy) and 'John Keel departed this life'. Indeed, throughout the entire Andover Circuit of about 500 members in that particular year, 143 had left for various reasons: eight had died, 59 had withdrawn voluntarily, sixteen had moved to other Circuits, and an astonishing 60 people had been 'excluded for criminality'.[34] Such a term, one assumes, was as applied according to the doctrines of the Church rather than the actual breaking of the law of the land. In the same report, a couple from Abbotts Ann were 'excluded, and preaching removed from their house' – further direct evidence that private houses were used for preaching in the absence of a chapel.

The first Superintendent Minister of Andover's chapel was the missionary who had first brought the movement to Andover, George Wallis. This post meant he had superiority over the other ministers and preachers allied to the Circuit. His salary for the three months ended June 1837 was £4/10/-. The other three preachers, Thomas Jackson, J. Tomplin and Henry Coles each received £4/-/-. Travelling allowances were also allocated, including one for George Wallis himself; evidently his duties did not just involve attending to the business of the Andover chapel; he also had to travel to the rural branches in order to preach.[35]

The system of preaching was minutely worked out so as to ensure that the ministers, the travelling preachers, the local preachers and the exhorters (the Primitive Methodist pecking order) were all given 'slots' in and around the Circuit to preach at set times and places. Many of these preachers were quite illiterate but though uneducated and untrained, they were able to speak effectively to an audience and had the potential to draw a crowd around them. Such a method with its variety of personalities helped to maintain interest and momentum, in both enthusing the already-converted and encouraging others to join the Church themselves. The 'preaching plan' was a pamphlet printed by local firms and was freely issued, setting out the precise programme in a table format for the following three months.[36] Code numbers were allocated to each preacher in order of status or reputation so that No.1 at the top was the Superintendent Minister, progressing down through all the levels to those at the bottom – the exhorters, the prayer leaders and finally, the auxiliaries. And if any preacher failed to meet his commitments without ensuring that somebody else was there to replace him, he was liable to lose his place on the plan or could suffer being dropped altogether. The minutes of Quarterly Meetings often consist largely of recommendations that particular individuals should go on or off the plan, or be moved from one place to another in the hierarchy.[37] No doubt the system promoted some healthy competition among the preachers, motivating them to perform well. But just as effectively, it helped to maintain the rigid discipline that was a feature of all the nonconformist persuasions.

We should attempt to look a little more closely at those involved with the new Andover Circuit. When George Wallis first walked into Andover on Sunday 5th May 1833, he was accompanied by supporters from the Bourne Valley whose interest had first been stirred by Thomas Russell two years before. Two of those most likely to have been with Wallis on that day were the brothers Richard and Michael Osmond, farmers of Linkenholt. Russell's memoir mentioned Michael giving him a shilling on his arrival in the village in 1831, and when the Andover Circuit was formed in 1837, Richard Osmond acted as its first secretary and his brother as a member of the first committee.[38] Later, when trustees were required for the Andover chapel in 1838, again Richard Osmond is named as one of the thirteen, as is also George Wallis. The others were a diverse mix: two artisans were carpenter George West and plasterer Thomas Short, both from Andover. A Longstock blacksmith, Jacob Martin, and James Noyce, a tailor from Abbotts Ann, also appear as do two woodmen from the Bourne Valley, John Page and William Holloway. Reflecting the social spread that Primitive Methodism attracted, two labourers, Richard Mitchener of Wherwell and William Stephens of Longstock, are also on the list. The final three are John Young, a carrier from Allington in Wiltshire; Andover stationer John King who lent £440 on a mortgage for the Andover chapel; and perhaps most surprisingly John Coster whose occupation is given as victualler;[39] the term can mean merely provisions, but as he was the licensee of the King's Head public house, it seems that at this moment the Temperance campaign had not entirely permeated the policy thinking of those in charge of the Andover Circuit. It is noticeable however, that when the time came for a new list of trustees to be compiled in 1840 when George Wallis had moved on, the publican's name is missing. The rest of the list remains largely unchanged except for the inclusion of a Mr Collins of Newbury who had lent £50 on the chapel house.[40]

As the 1840s progressed, the strength of the Andover Circuit increased and by 1849 it had built 17 chapels. The Andover chapel had cost £490 but those built in the villages were smaller versions, reflecting the level of population they were expected to serve: Amport's cost just over £144 in 1846, while in the same year, one erected at Longstock cost only £36. The two village communities were estimated at 764 and 200 respectively.[41] Even the smallest chapels often commissioned tea-ware from the Staffordshire potteries with the individual branch to which it belonged printed on its surface, an indication that the chapel was not regarded exclusively as a place for holy worship, but could be a centre for social gathering and fund-raising events. What was achieved is quite staggering when one considers that in only four of these places did branch membership exceed 30 people. Many saw numbers well under 20, and in Allington a chapel was built in 1843 with a membership there of just seven people out of a population of 95.[42] Obviously the Circuit system which ensured the pooling of resources was vital in allowing the Connexion to spread into the rural areas.

The Primitive Methodist Chapel in Sarson Lane, Amport, early 20th cent. It was rebuilt in 1928.

There were diverting moments when the zeal for improvement reached comic proportions, such as in 1864 when the two local ministers, Henry Yeates and Aaron Smith put forward a motion which they hoped would be adopted by the District Meeting of Conference, together with their reasons for doing so:

> That none of our ministers and local preachers should be allowed to officiate among us who wear a moustache:
>
> 1) Because it assumes a military rather than the ministerial character.
> 2) Because it is conformity to the world and the Gospel says "Be ye transformed."
> 3) Because preachers should be examples to their hearers and those preachers are bad models for imitation to sacred things.
> 4) Because numbers in our societies and congregations have signified their disapprobation of receiving such preachers.[43]

We might judge that at the root of all this was that same puritanical streak that had adopted Temperance with such enthusiasm, a hankering to hinder and control merely for its own sake, in an effort to suppress freedom. No doubt it is this inherent part of the movement's character that has left us today with a rather jaundiced impression of its one-time adherents. We have a sense that they were rather stern-faced, serious and narrow-minded, generally suspicious of people enjoying themselves. There may well have been an element of religious zealotry, but it is far from the overall truth; indeed for most church members their enthusiasm was joyous and the marches and camp meetings were, within limits, occasions for partying.

Whether the rise in membership of all the nonconformist churches during the nineteenth century was catalyst or symptom, the crusade for a higher standard of morality moved in tandem with the great Victorian changes that social legislation and industrial progress implemented. What has been termed the age of improvement manifested itself not only in material, social and imperial advance, but also in a spiritual one - or at least in what was then considered so. Though society was far from perfect, the increase in elementary education for all (long in advance of Forster's Education Act of 1870) encouraged a broader outlook, and with developments in communications such as the railways, the penny post and the proliferation of local newspapers, a national opinion evolved based on a consensus of honourable standards. Improvements in public health, the reform of factory law and the strong ethical outlook of many of those in business were all part of a movement that nourished and replenished itself. Central in all this was a popular quest for religious and moral validity, accessible to all. Primitive Methodism, for all its faults and inconsistencies, did much social good, bringing to those isolated village communities a new involvement removed from work and the local inn. It believed in the nobleness of the human spirit and that virtuous pursuits could bring their own reward.

Maybe it was all too fragile to last long, but the ideology survived more or less intact into the new century. The centenary of the Connexion's formation, deemed to date from the first Mow Cop camp meeting, was celebrated in 1907. Commemorative plates were produced to celebrate the occasion, on the back of which it was claimed that chapels and preaching places numbered 4,905, and church members 210,173. The Andover Circuit was still growing and in 1909 a separate Test Valley branch seceded from it. In the following year this became the Hurstbourne Tarrant Circuit, incorporating many of the old-established branches linked to Andover. But the Armageddon that was the First World War splintered and shattered Primitive Methodism as it did so much else. The generation that served in the trenches and who saw the savagery and the meaningless slaughter at first hand, could no longer put their faith and trust in the pre-war values that had once been easy to accept; for them, everything had changed and things were never going to be the same again. With three quarters of a million British dead and some towns and villages losing virtually all its sons, the blind faith of an earlier period was irreparably damaged. Primitive Methodism declined like all the individual religions during the years of war and, although managing to retain its membership in absolute terms, certainly fell if measured as a proportion of the rising population during the 1920s.[44] In 1932, the main national Methodist Connexions decided to sink their differences and merge together.[45] Though technically aligned, there was still some

Two images of the destruction of the East Street Methodist Chapel, 1967.

local autonomy for a while and the Andover Primitive Methodist Circuit became Andover East Street Circuit, to distinguish itself from the Wesleyan Circuit chapel in Bridge Street. But declining membership was a harsh reality which the Second World War could only reinforce. In 1937 the relatively new (1910) Hurstbourne Tarrant Circuit merged with the Andover Wesleyan Circuit and in 1948 the Micheldever Primitive Methodist Circuit, established in 1835, also joined these two, to form the Andover Trinity Circuit. Finally, in 1951 the East Street Circuit abandoned its degree of independence and merged with Andover Trinity to form the Andover Circuit. The East Street chapel struggled on in a limited way for a few more years but the old building was characterised by neglect and creeping decay.

Today, the modern motorist travelling along one of the main thoroughfares of Andover drives right over the site of the 1838 chapel. Both the chapel and the congregation that sustained it have gone out of fashion and life has moved on. The hopes and enthusiasms of 1838 became victim to the 1960s town development bulldozer that also promised so much. Every age approaches its problems in different ways with varying degrees of success, and in judging Primitive Methodism as a movement we should acknowledge the achievements: it helped to rein in the nineteenth century scourge of drunkenness, immeasurably enriched the lives of individuals and improved the morale of whole communities in an age that had not yet embraced national responsibility for social welfare. Primitive Methodism did not prevent starvation, relieve the horror of unemployment or keep people from being turned out of their homes; but it lifted the spirit, gave purpose to its members and reinforced the idea of a public conscience. In doing all that, they also had fun.

Post-war Britain with its radical shifts in science, private motoring, social policy and outlook made much of what had gone on before seem archaic and inappropriate. New gods replaced the old and when the newly-formed Welfare State promised boldly to care for its citizens 'from the cradle to the grave', people could not help but turn their heads in a different direction; where once they looked to their church, they would in future look to their government.

References

1. Davies, Rupert, George, A. R., and Rupp, Gordon, eds., *A History of the Methodist Church of Great Britain*, 4 vols. (London 1963-88).
2. Hobsbawm, E.J., and Rude, George, *Captain Swing*. (1969).
3. HRO 132A01/2, Russell, Thomas, *Primitive Methodism in Berkshire*. (1885).
4. *ibid.*
5. Watts, Michael, *The Dissenters*, Vol. II, 1791-1859. (1995).
6. Rolt, L.T.C., *Waterloo Iron Works: A History of Taskers of Andover, 1809-1968*. (1969).
7. Paintin, Bernard, *Since Wesley came to Andover*. (1951).
8. Bebbington, D.W., *Evangelicalism in Modern Britain: A History from the 1730s to the 1980s*. (1989).
9. Paintin, Bernard, *Since Wesley came to Andover*. (1951).

10. HRO 132A01/3, Brinkworth Synod Report, 1932.
11. Paintin, Bernard, *Since Wesley Came to Andover.* (1951).
12. *ibid.*
13. HRO 96M72/NMC/A23, Circuit Accounts, 1837-1851.
14. *ibid.*
15. Bebbington, D.W., *Evangelicalism in Modern Britain: A History from the 1730s to the 1980s.* (1989).
16. Vickers, John, ed., *The Religious Census of Hampshire 1851.* H.C.C. (1993).
17. HRO 96M72/NMC/A23, Circuit Accounts, 1837-1851.
18. HRO 96M72/NMC/B28, Quarterly Meetings Account Book, 1840-1852.
19. HRO 96M72/NMC/R7, Primitive Methodist Baptism Register, 1834-1873.
20. Brown, Kenneth D., *A Social History of the Nonconformist Ministry.* (1988).
21. HRO 96M72/NMC/R7, Primitive Methodist Baptism Register, 1834-1873.
22. HRO 96M72/NMC/A23, Circuit Accounts, 1837-1851.
23. Watts, Michael, *The Dissenters*, Vol. II, 1791-1859. (1995).
24. HRO 96M72/NMC/B28, Quarterly Meetings Account Book, 1840-1852.
25. Watts, Michael, *The Dissenters*, Vol. II, 1791-1859. (1995).
26. Bebbington, D.W., *Evangelicalism in Modern Britain: A History from the 1730s to the 1980s.* (1989).
27. Brown, Kenneth D., *A Social History of the Nonconformist Ministry.* (1988).
28. HRO 96M72/NMC/R7, Primitive Methodist Baptism Register, 1834-1873.
29. HRO 42M83/2, Congregational Church Minute Book, 1832.
30. Bebbington, D.W., *Evangelicalism in Modern Britain: A History from the 1730s to the 1980s.* (1989).
31. Watts, Michael, *The Dissenters*, Vol. II, 1791-1859. (1995).
32. The Temperance Hall in Andover was built in 1868. In 1872 a group of Wesleyan Methodists left the chapel because they were dissatisfied with their leadership's weak stance with regard to abstinence, and held meetings in the Temperance Hall.
33. Watts, Michael, *The Dissenters*, Vol. II, 1791-1859. (1995).
34. HRO 96M72/B41, Circuit Report. 1848.
35. HRO 96M72/NMC/A23, Circuit Accounts, 1837-1851.
36. Copies of the Preaching Plans are filed with the Circuit Reports at HRO.
37. HRO 96M72/NMC/B28, Quarterly Meetings, 1837-1860.
38. HRO 96M72/NMC/A23, Circuit Accounts, 1837-1851.
39. ibid.
40. HRO 96M72/NMC/A9, Quarterly Meetings Account Book, 1840-1852.
41. HRO 96M72/ NMC/B41, 1849 Circuit Report.
42. ibid.
43. HRO 96M72/NMC/B41, Circuit Report 1864.
44. Davies, Rupert, George, A.R., and Rupp, Gordon, eds., *A History of the Methodist Church of Great Britain*, 4 vols. (London 1963-88).
45. Three Methodist religions merged in 1932: The Wesleyans who had 517,551 members and 8,152 chapels, the Primitive Methodists with 222,021 members and 4,356 chapels, and the United Methodists with 179,551 members and 2,900 chapels. The Independent Methodists and the Wesleyan Support Union remained independent and between them could muster approx. 25,000 members.

LAYTON'S OF ANDOVER

THE HISTORY OF A CHINA AND GLASS WAREHOUSE

1853 – 1952

David J. Borrett

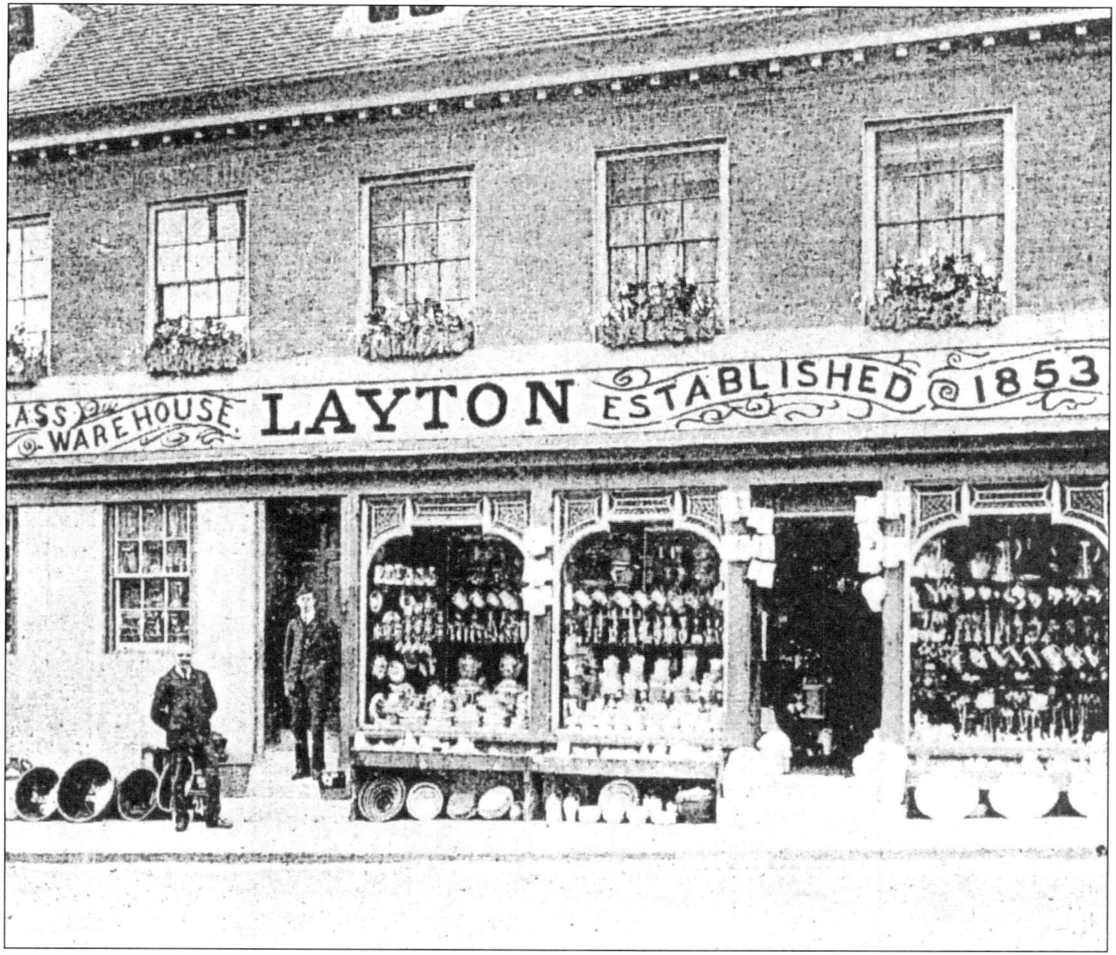

The front of Rosa Layton's china shop, before 1907.

The old line of shops that once stood behind the Guildhall was demolished in the late 1960s to make way for Town Development. One of the most attractive was the well-known premises on the eastern corner, popularly remembered as Scott's shoe shop. The decorative brickwork façade of the structure is visible in many photographs of the High Street, as are the buildings at the other end of the row. However, the several shops that lay behind the Guildhall rarely attracted the photographer's eye, except in 1967 when Charles Wardell undertook the task of producing a series of shots of the old part of the town, including several views of this particular line of buildings. It was a last look round just before the bulldozers moved in.[1]

Immediately next to Scott's was a classic Georgian building of quiet market town style, rather similar to some of those still surviving in East Street. By 1967, it had been the greengrocery of Reg. Elwick for about 15 years, and before that, for a very short time, the premises of a relative of his, a Mr Booth, whose own greengrocery tenure ended abruptly after his criminal involvement with stolen motor vehicles became the subject of legal proceedings. The episode was in stark contrast to the continuity of previous years, as prior to that No 49 High Street had long been home to the china and glass emporium known as Rosa E. Layton, a family enterprise that had been established in 1853.

The building's outer façade was predominantly of early nineteenth century origin, having a tiled roof with three evenly-spaced dormer windows above a dentil frieze. Five sliding sash windows lined the red-bricked upper floor while at ground floor level (in 1967) there were three shop windows, separated by two single doorways, each with two stone steps. The shop window at the western end of the building was a late addition and replaced two sash windows, similar to those in the storey above. Until then, this part of the building, together with the adjacent door, was part of the living accommodation. These alterations were carried out some time during the first half of the twentieth century – certainly after 1907.[2]

Zaccheus Layton, who first established the china and glass business there, was a native of Aylesbury, born in 1816. The name Layton was a local one to that area, and early spellings can be traced as Laighton, Leyghton and Layghton in sixteenth and seventeenth century parish records, becoming standardised as Layton by the eighteenth century. In 1811 Zaccheus Layton's parents were married in the parish church of St Mary's Aylesbury. Evidently they were nonconformists as each successive child – all boys – were baptised at Hale Leys Independent Chapel (the law did not then allow marriage in unlicensed buildings such as nonconformist chapels and dissenters had to marry in the parish church). But misfortune seemed to strike the Layton parents over the name John. The first, baptised in 1820, died as an infant, and then a second given the same name, baptised in 1824, suffered the same fate. This double tragedy might have been the reason why the Laytons had a change of religious heart, for they subsequently withdrew their allegiance to the Independent Chapel and returned to

Anglicanism. This was publicly demonstrated by all the surviving children being baptised for a second time at the parish church of St. Mary's on 23rd August 1829.

By the mid 1840s, Zaccheus had married Hannah and was living in Newbury. Three children were born there, William, Robert and Louisa (Lucy), before the family moved to Andover in about 1852-3 when Walter was born. The 1861 census for Andover lists two further children, Frank aged seven and Arthur aged three, although Walter is then absent from the family home. Zaccheus is described as an *earthenware* dealer. This suggests a more utilitarian type of stock-in-trade at this point, although it may have just been the census enumerator's blanket term. The Post Office directory for 1867 lists Zaccheus as a china and glass dealer, as do later directories, but here too we cannot be sure that the term was not an in-house one, applied to all such trades. When first setting up business we might expect Zaccheus to begin with domestic ware which would not have cost so much to stock, and then develop into more expensive lines if trade proved successful. But at the same time he would have continued to sell the cheaper goods as well; in a small town the kitchen was just as important, if not more so, than the drawing room, and an astute businessman would not have forgotten that there was money to be made from pots as well as porcelain. Indeed, years later, when the business was well-established, the shop continued to supply wares of diverse quality and level because there was a healthy demand for all.

As the children grew up they seem to have scattered. Robert moved to Whitechapel, London, married Eliza and sired three children, but by 1873 the family was back in Andover, with Robert running what was then known commonly as a marine store, at 87 High Street. He was more precisely described as a 'wholesale and retail rag, bone and metal merchant, and a coal merchant' in a directory of 1880, but by 1889 was a greengrocer, a trade in which he stayed engaged until the shop was taken over by Alfred Gorey about the beginning of the First World War. The six children attended Miss Gale's Infant School.[3]

Another of Zaccheus' children who left and then returned to the town was Walter, who would eventually succeed his father as proprietor of the china and glass business at No 49 High Street. Apprenticed as a cabinet maker, the 1871 census lists him as 18 years old and living with the family above the shop. The other family occupants were Louisa, then 19, Frank, an apprentice carpenter, and 13 year-old Arthur. Zaccheus was now aged 54 and Hannah, his wife, 46. Ten years later, in 1881, Hannah was dead and all the children had left home. Only Zaccheus remained, with a housekeeper, a domestic servant and a lodger installed.

Families may disperse in all directions but Walter had gone farther than most. He does not appear on the 1881 census because he was almost certainly in the United States where he was married, and then widowed. The brief union produced one daughter, Jenny. In 1889, Zaccheus died, and by then Walter had returned to Andover, as he took over the running of the shop. His daughter who lived with him was then aged five.

On 7th April 1890, in a civil ceremony, Walter married Rosa Elizabeth Banks, a 27 year-old governess whose late mother had derived her income from the possession of several local properties, the revenue from which was shared between Rosa and her brother William. Her father who had died years before was James Banks, a coal merchant of Bridge Street. Rosa was not poor and she was possessed of a good business brain. Although the 36 year-old Walter was almost 10 years her senior, it may have seemed a good match. It is difficult to know exactly when Walter returned to the town and whether he was running the shop prior to his father's death. Possibly Rosa had been Jenny's governess; her home address was just across the street from Walter's, near the entrance to Union Street; being so close to Walter's shop, she would have made the ideal choice if a governess had been sought to look after Jenny.

The marriage produced two children – Leslie Banks in 1891 and Gladys Charlotte in 1892 who both attended Gale's School for a short time before being sent to a private school in 1899. The shop which Walter ran, and Rosa helped to finance, was apparently successful. A commercial review of the business written about 1891 pays tribute to the new proprietor in glowing terms:

> Since Mr Walter Layton succeeded to the business it has been conducted on the old lines, but with renewed vigour and enterprise, with the result that it now stands at the head of similar concerns in Andover...The stocks are exceedingly fine and...all the leading manufacturers and makers are well-represented, including Minton, Worcester, Staffordshire, Derby, Wedgwood and Copeland. Every taste and every requirement in this direction has been fully catered for and a copiousness of selection is offered that leaves nothing to be desired. The leading lines...are dinner, tea and dessert services, in every style and at all prices, toilet and chamber sets, plates, dishes, jugs, artistic-cut table glass, decanters, flower-stands, bowls, English, French, and Dresden fancy goods, and a full line of general and useful earthenware. Doulton's famous art pottery is shown in large variety, and the establishment is replete with superior goods, suitable for holiday and wedding presents. Mr Layton buys his articles first-hand and in the best markets, securing every advantage in the matter of price that can result from large orders judiciously placed...All kinds of goods are lent on hire for school treats, private parties, and public banquets. The trade is both wholesale and retail, the patronage of the house comprising the leading families, hotel proprietors, and licensed victuallers, and the smaller shopkeepers of the district. Mr Layton is an able, intelligent, and pushing tradesman, fair and honourable in all his dealings, and commanding the confidence of all who come into business relations with him.[4]

Walter's qualities as a shopkeeper and general purveyor of goodwill undoubtedly impressed the reviewer, but life above the shop did not present quite the same picture; wherever and however the difficulties surfaced, Rosa and Walter's marriage soon began to crumble, and by 1895 plans were being drawn up to effect a legal separation.

The subsequent Minutes of Arrangement gave Rosa custody of the children and the tenancy of the shop. In return she agreed to pay Walter his share of the assets of the business, after making allowance for the book debts (those who owed the business for goods taken on account). It appears that Walter had already borrowed the sum of £274/18/4d from Rosa, so this was also deducted from the final amount paid over.[5] An indenture made on the 8th January 1896 states that a valuation of the assets carried out by Allan Herbert was calculated at £1,376/9/8d, from which was deducted the loan and the book debts, leaving £716/13/10d to be divided between them.[6] From this moment on, both Walter and his daughter Jenny seem to vanish.[7] Possibly they returned to America.

Under Rosa's stewardship, the shop flourished as she adapted her trade to cater for the changing circumstances of the age. By the turn of the century, travelling had become a national pursuit and a profitable development for china dealers up and down the country was the sale of novelties printed with the borough crest or a local scene, for sale to day trippers and tourists. These were specially commissioned from the Staffordshire factories in a variety of standard shapes ranging from miniature vases and animals through to models of transport and household gadgets. Attractively priced, crested and pictorial china ornaments were not only bought by visitors, but also by the town's inhabitants. Soon Rosa was styling herself as "Agent for Foley Andover Arms China". Foley was the trade name of one of the more prolific factories producing such wares, and an added advantage in selling this was that Rosa could advertise the business; each was marked underneath with the legend "Rosa E. Layton, 49 High St, Andover".

An advertisement of 1907 incorporates a rare view of Layton's business premises.[8] This was prior to the alteration which provided another shop window to the left, but the length of the overhead sign-writing shows clearly that the unaltered section was nonetheless part of the same premises. Outside are displayed stoneware crocks and jars, and farther along, some large meat dishes of ordinary Staffordshire quality. In the windows, there seems to be a vast array of jugs, many in graduated sets which were also standard household ware. Just discernible is a variety of stoneware hunting jugs, popular at this period, which were issued by Royal Doulton in two tones of brown and applied with various sporting motifs. The open door fails to reveal any detail of exactly what was inside but it is evident that the shop was well-stocked with goods laid out from floor level upwards. Possibly Rosa departed a little from the path that her husband had tried to follow when he stocked the wares of the 'leading manufacturers'. From Rosa's point of view, although it may have been prestigious to display the finest Minton, Worcester, Derby and Spode, and undoubtedly there were many families in the area with sufficient wealth to purchase it, perhaps the shop's accounts suggested that the balance was out of kilter for an ordinary market town like Andover. There was a profusion of other factories in the Potteries which, though less eminent, could supply excellent china at a cheaper price, and a good mixture of qualities and price may well have been a more viable commercial proposition. However, perhaps it would be wrong to overplay any differences in trading style between Walter and Rosa; the fulsome language of the 1891 review suggests that the writer would likely exaggerate the more up-market side of the business while choosing to pass over its less impressive, workaday elements. And customer demand in 1907 may not have been quite the same as that of 1891. Consumer fashions were as potent then as they are today.

The 1907 advertisement shows that the business was, in the language of the day, a 'china and glass warehouse', both wholesale and retail. Rosa claimed that she was a contractor for His Majesty's Government (probably she supplied the expanding military presence in the area) and, as in Walter's day, goods, including cutlery and silver, could be lent on hire. In addition, glass and china repairs were undertaken, probably by the use of metal rivets, and often said to have been the work of the travelling gypsies. No doubt Rosa had regular callers and contacts, travellers or not, who would do such work. Evidently, there was more to the business than simple retailing and Rosa's formula must have been an effective one for her pre-eminence in Andover was long held, and during her time no other similar establishment set up in direct competition. Admittedly, Parsons and Hart whose trade was house furnishing, might include china and glass in one of their departments; and the family business of Holmes, the publishers of the *Andover Advertiser,* sold ceramic ware as part of their stock of fancy goods, but it would be wrong to think either of these were china and glass dealers per se. Only Rosa E. Layton could lay claim to that.

Unfortunately, it is only near the end of Rosa's time that we can be on firmer ground in pinpointing more precisely some of the aspects of her business practice. Three day books, charting the period from 1931 to 1943, survive among the records at Winchester Record Office, deposited by the Clerk of the Works in 1970, after the premises had been consigned to rubble - probably a last-minute find by the contractors when preparing to build the new town centre.[9] The period covered by these books mark a time both of national and personal upheaval. Possibly by the early 1930s Rosa had passed on the running of the shop to her son Leslie Banks Layton; her later years were beset by prolonged illness, and after her death on 13th February 1936, aged 75, the business was continued by Leslie, without any noticeable interruption. During the period Rosa had been proprietor, from 1896 onwards, the population of Andover had been steadily increasing, rising from just over 6000 people to reach over 10,000 by the 1930s. The favourable expansion of both people and houses was obviously a contributing factor to the shop's success and at some point Rosa had also purchased the freehold of the building.

From the names of the firms with which the shop dealt in the 1930s, it is easier to assess the type of stock. Certainly there was still much that was utilitarian: T. G. Green, Grindley and Co. and Bovey Tracey Pottery produced kitchenalia and dinnerware of ordinary quality while more decorative objects, albeit mass-produced for the lower end of the market, were turned out by factories such as Hancock and Sons and Burgess Bros. Typical were sets of graduated jugs, pairs of vases and dessert wares of printed designs on an earthenware body that was overlaid with cheap gilding.

Leslie Banks Layton, c.1908.

Another factory with which Rosa did business was the works at Aller Vale who made terra-cotta country pottery of red Devon clay painted with such motifs as cockerels, mottoes and cottages. Dealings were also with firms such as Plant and Co, Shelley and Aynsley which were then considered secondary manufacturers of finer quality products. Familiar names such as Wedgwood, Copeland and Royal Doulton also appear in Rosa's accounts; by the 1930s, each of these firms had reached a zenith of output that encompassed a vast range including earthenware services of standard printed patterns, artist-designed hand-crafted stoneware and top quality, individually-painted and signed cabinet porcelain of rich ground colours and raised gilding. Rosa might have chosen to stock any of this; the obvious diversity of her enterprise would no doubt have tempted her to include at least a smattering of what was both sumptuous and expensive. Aside from china and glass, Layton's seem to have sold brooms and mops too as there are regular sales of these on account during the 1930s. Perhaps they had a good source of supply and were able to undercut everyone else.

Manufacturers and suppliers of glassware are also recorded: J. Wuidart were Belgian importers with warehouses at Bartlett's Buildings in London from whom Rosa could have ordered a range of products without having to deal with individual firms.

Both British and foreign products could be bought from them at competitive prices, and the innovative glass made by James Powell and Sons, marketed as Whitefriars, was a staple line during the 1930s. The firm of Jobling and Co was a manufacturer with which Rosa dealt directly. A popular product for them during this period was opalescent and blue tinted moulded glass in imitation of Lalique. Cut glass was supplied by either Edinburgh and Reith or Thomas Webb while some of the pressed glass came from the factory of Davidson and Co of Gateshead. Everything arrived at the shop in crates which were sent back by rail. Cheques were periodically written out to individual firms in settlement of accounts. Sometimes, items were not delivered or they arrived broken in which case adjustments had to be made.

Many of Rosa's customers, especially if they were either fellow traders or regular purchasers, kept running accounts. In those days, before the advent of chain stores and nationally-based concerns, high street business was provided by independent, local people operating in a relatively small way. In order that each could thrive, the collective interest was best served by local money being kept within the confines of the local circle, and so each dutifully patronised the other. It was not just a question of convenience and loyalty, but a sound principle for survival. So we see that a bicycle was purchased from F. Harvey of No 78 High Street for £8/12/6d, presumably for deliveries, and whenever Mr Harvey required replacements for china that was broken or perhaps needed to purchase a suitable wedding present, he went to Layton's. It may be coincidence but when in December 1942 Leslie sent a cheque for £1/1/- to the Mayor's Christmas Fund, five days later the Mayoress, Mrs Bell, came in and bought a set of toilet ware for 15/11d. In the mid 1930s Dr Hodgson purchased a tea service for 11/6d, as did Mr Crang a lesser one. The latter, a local ironmonger, received a discount of 10d on his 8/6d. T. Lynn and Sons were frequent customers, and as an example of how in those days people could obtain replacements without spending more than was strictly necessary, we see that Mrs Buckland, wife of the proprietor of the large draper's shop just around the corner in Upper High Street, was supplied with a vegetable dish made to fit her existing cover for 5/11d.

Account transactions were often of small value. Just because people were relatively wealthy did not mean they regularly spent large sums: on 23rd February 1932, the Countess of Portsmouth bought 1 "Yuan" (a standard blue and white pattern made by Woods) saucer for 5d and 2 tea plates for 10d, while on the 26th August, Mrs T. Webb (wife of one of the Freemen of the Borough) bought three 2lb jampots at 6½d each. The Hon. Bryan Guinness of Biddesden House, whose wife had been the former Diana Mitford, was also a client whose name regularly appears in the records for diverse orders of small value. All such purchases were recorded for settlement at a later date. Of course there were also cash sales, but these did not require any special treatment except the total amount being entered for each day.

The 1930s was a difficult period for retailing. Sales on account for the financial year that ended 31st March 1932 were £636/13/5d. Without records for previous years it is impossible to gauge how good or bad this was. Certainly it was much better than the following year when account sales dipped to £464/10/2d. 1933-34 was little better at £486/10/2d. From then on things improved slowly and by March 1937 the sales on account that year had reached £619/13/-. Cash sales varied tremendously from day to day. Fridays were often the best while Wednesdays, which would have been mornings only, were quiet. Anything between £1 and £10 seems to have been a normal daily take, with £3 to £6 being a reasonable average. Perhaps the figures between 1932 and 1936 owe something to Rosa's withdrawal from the business through illness, and are not wholly attributable to the effects of the economic slump.

After Rosa's death, the business was continued by her son Leslie who styled himself L. Banks Layton, although the shop kept its business name of Rosa E. Layton. He was still a bachelor and may have been employed by his mother all his working life. Indeed, it may well be the 16-year-old Leslie who is standing on the doorstep in the 1907 advertisement. The older gentleman in the picture, though looking very much like a proprietor, is probably Rosa's manager rather than Walter who had then long since separated from his wife.[10]

The middle of the 1930s was marked by Royal celebrations: the Silver Jubilee of King George V and Queen Mary, the proposed Coronation of King Edward VIII and the actual Coronation of King George VI and Queen Elizabeth. With each successive event, china dealers could rely on the sale of commemorative wares produced for the occasion. The abdication of Edward VIII, although five months before the planned coronation date, did not prevent the sale of a vast quantity of mugs, plates, cups and saucers and other sundry articles to private purchasers, all manufactured and in the shops well in advance. For both factories and dealers, the constitutional upset was by no means a total loss as most people probably bought similar wares again for the Coronation of King George VI, scheduled for the same date – 12th May 1937. In Andover, as elsewhere, the Borough Council issued mugs to all the children of the town, both in 1935 and 1937, inscribed with Andover and the name of the Mayor, B. Shaw Porter, who was in office on both occasions. The cost of each local celebration, including the purchase of mugs for the children, was raised through the Council levying an extra 1d on the rates. Disappointingly for Rosa E. Layton however, though the business should have been ideally placed to supply the mugs, there is no record in the day books of any transaction to this effect, so it seems the Council must have dealt directly with the manufacturer.[11] Of course the Council had to be sure to secure the commemorative mugs at an economical price as they were spending ratepayers' money.

Despite passing over Layton's to supply the mugs, the Mayor, B. Shaw Porter, was a regular customer; whenever he proposed to hold a large dinner or tea, he hired the requisite china. For example on 24th December 1936, 230 tea-cups, saucers and tea-plates, and 100 medium plates, together with three large jugs were ordered at a total hire cost of 15/11d. A fortnight later more crockery was hired for a smaller occasion. Cutlery was also available and Mrs Portsmouth ordered 154 large forks and 139 dessert spoons, together with 36 large jugs the week following the coronation at a cost of 16/9d. Breakages and shortfalls were charged after their return - 5d for a tea-plate and 2/- for a jug.

The business must have sold a great deal of commemorative china during the celebrations, and there were evidently several varieties on sale in the shop. Just before Jubilee day in 1935, Mrs Yorke Scarlett bought 31 mugs and 28 cups, saucers and plates, spending a total of £2/13/4d, while Mrs Elmes bought 36 mugs at 10/6d a dozen. An advertisement which ran for many weeks on the front page of the local newspaper in 1937 informed the reader that a range of 'Coronation china' was now available at Layton's. A week before the event, Mrs T. Clark bought two mugs at 9d each while Mrs Elmes this time bought just six at 6d and Mrs Hartigan bought another six at 3d each. Hartigans was a well-known local racing stables so perhaps the mugs were for the stable lads These were all relatively inexpensive versions, but there were better examples on offer. Mrs McCleod bought a mug for 1/9d and a tobacco jar for 3/6d. The bone china cup and saucer illustrated, manufactured by Plant and Co of Longton, would have cost several shillings. Certainly it was purchased at Layton's because it bears a paper label to that effect underneath.

Coronation cup and saucer, 1937.

Notes at the beginning of the daybooks detail some of the annual insurances which had to be paid: £2/12/6d was enough to cover £1500 of stock (an indication of the stock level at that time) while 17/6d covered employees. The premium for windows was set at £1/5/- while the value of the premises, then estimated at £4,500, required £4/10/-. Insurances were also paid on dwellings around the town for which Rosa, and later Leslie, received rent. Some of these were likely purchased years before by Rosa's father and included Nos. 9 and 13 Vigo Road, 17 and 41 West Street, one house in London Street, and another dwelling in Adelaide Road. However, newer houses like 26 and 28 Charlton Road and also 113 Old Winton Road, must have been bought by Rosa herself.[12] It seems if business warranted it, she invested surplus money into buying to let.

There were other regular expenses: an advertisement in the *Andover Parish Magazine* cost 9/- annually, while 200lbs of 40 x 48 brown paper for wrapping, was purchased at 14/- cwt. An advertisement in *Kelly's Directory of Andover* for two years was £2/10/- while a listing in *Kelly's Directory of Hampshire* was 7/- for four years. And a regular subscription to the *Pottery Gazette* at 15/- kept Rosa and Leslie in regular touch with innovations and fashions in the industry. In order to further the chance of attracting new customers, in 1933 the shop was advertising in the programmes issued by the New Theatre (later the Rex cinema) in West Street at 1/- a month. However, in 1938, Leslie was refused an advert in the chapel magazine, and on 4th June 1940, his regular placing in the *Andover Advertiser* was cancelled by him because the charge had increased by 16/3d.[13]

In the early years of war, there seems to have been a difficulty in keeping staff: 'Smith', who had joined as a 16-year-old in December 1932, left in June 1940 to join up. Leslie then hired 15-year-old Bertie Leonard Hallett who left after two weeks, followed by F. H. James Leader who was taken on in the middle of July and left before the middle of August. On April 21st 1941, Henry Tully, aged 17, of 54 South Street, started but finished within a week! Leslie was more successful with Len Smith who was taken on in May 1941 and stayed eighteen months until November 1942, followed by Harold Ayres Cook who remained until September 1943.[14] Although the war was on, in none of these cases were the boys old enough for statutory conscription; we might conclude that while 'Smith' had suited him well enough and may of course have been tutored by Rosa, Leslie could be a tough employer on those not familiar with his way of doing things.

During the war, many factories ceased production altogether, while some (government-sanctioned) made goods purely intended for export. Anything produced for the domestic market was devoid of colour or restricted to a few drab-looking tones. Leslie noted in the daybook in April 1942 the 'Houses good for supplying in Wartime'. These included Doulton & Co, Wild & Sons, Grindley's, Wilkinson, Rankin & Co, Plant, Meakin, Howard Pottery and New Hall Pottery. A useful sale in December 1942 was that of twelve teapots to the R.A.F. Sergeants' Mess at 4/9d each, and at the end of the following January, Mrs Cope from the White Hart Hotel in Bridge street purchased casseroles, glass jugs, a cruet and eight glass spoons for a total of £1/19/ 8d. Although the war ended in 1945, the severe restrictions on production continued to be imposed for many years and it was not until the early 1950s that colour again began to creep back into home market crockery.

Those who thought Leslie a confirmed old bachelor must have been surprised in 1947 when he married Mrs Doreen Lavinia Riley, a widow with two teenage daughters. Initially, they lived above the shop at 49 High Street, but eventually it was decided to close the shop and move to a house in Junction Road. Leslie was now 60 and he opted for retirement. He retained ownership of the shop which became the greengrocery run by Reg Elwick. This remained so until Town Development forced the closure and demolition of all the shops both behind the Guildhall and in the West Street area. The condemned buildings were all compulsorily purchased in 1964 by Andover Borough Council.[15] Leslie's widow carried out the conveyance as he had died three years earlier on 29th August 1961. However, the plans for Town Development had been officially drawn up before his death and he is said to have been saddened by his old family premises' likely demise.[16]

49 Market Place, Andover, 1967.

Closing in 1952, Layton's had been established in Andover for 99 years. Only a few Andover businesses have surpassed that length of tenure.[17] The gap in the market was filled by The China Mart which was located at No 1 London Street and The Pottery Shop in Bridge Street, but by the early 1970s only T. Lynn & Sons, principally ironmongers, and also to a small degree, Holmes and Sons, were dealing in high-class china and glass. The other two specialists had disappeared.

In recent years, demand for more standard ware was filled by Timothy Whites, now defunct, and one or two others which included it as part of a general stock. The privately-run concern known as Chantry China, originally in Union Street and at present near the top of the Upper High Street, is alone in retailing better quality goods - just one shop to serve a population of over 35,000 people. One suspects Rosa, given such a potential clientele, would have been rubbing her hands with glee.

References

1. A set of these photographs are deposited in Andover Reference Library.
2. An illustration of the building before alteration appears in *Hampshire and the Isle of Wight by Pen and Camera*, published by William Mate and Sons Ltd. (1907) (Winchester Reference Library, POO1468995, Class SH12, No.10692).
3. HRO 208M86/1-3, Gale's School Admission Register.
4. *Industrial Great Britain, A Commercial Review of Leading Firms Selected from Important Towns of England*, London Printing and Engraving Company n.d. (c.1891).
5. HRO 46M84, Box 70, Minutes of Arrangement, 16th December 1895, between Walter Layton and Rosa Elizabeth Layton.
6. HRO 46M84, Box 70, Indenture, 8th January 1896.
7. Neither appears in the online 1901 Census of England and Wales, nor is Walter's death registered before that year. Moreover, at the time of his daughter Gladys Charlotte's marriage in 1913, he is presumably still living as the certificate states, under father of the bride: 'Walter Layton, china merchant', without the addition of the usual '(deceased)'.
8. *Hampshire and Isle of Wight by Pen and Camera*, William Mate and Sons. (1907).
9. HRO 90M70/B1-2-3. Day Books, 1931-43.
10. When Rosa came to draw up her will in 1934, she left a bequest to her manager.
11. The 1935 mugs I have seen have no manufacturers stamp, but the 1937 versions are marked Grimwade's Royal Winton.
12. Rosa's brother, William James Banks who died in 1926, left some properties to her in his will.
13. HRO 90M70/B1-2-3. Day Books, 1931-43.
14. ibid.
15. Documents relating to compulsory purchases by Andover Borough Council. Their reference: HP 74185. Beech Hurst Council Offices.
16. Information supplied by Miss June M. Harris.
17. Retail businesses that were long-lived include: Shaw and Sons, Harvey's, Holmes', Lynn's, Pearse's, and Parsons and Hart.

ANDOVER COTTAGE HOSPITAL

Andrew Jackson

Introduction

Nowadays, cradle to the grave health care is there for the asking. Advances in medical science show no signs of slackening, illnesses both real and imaginary are treated by a bewildering array of treatments, there are hospital beds and surgeons perform the most incredible operations on the human body. And for the past 60 years this has been free.

Many people can remember the time when health care was not free, when the doctor's bill, which had to be paid quarterly, was a major item and payment had to be planned carefully. This meant that many illnesses simply went untreated because the money was not there to pay.

Hospitals were being founded in large towns from the 18th century; thus in Winchester the County Hospital dates from 1736. Increasing numbers of voluntary hospitals were being founded in smaller towns during the first half of the 19th century, often with the support of a generous titled person but backed by other essential local interest and money.

The first cottage hospital was started in Cranley in Surrey in 1859. The Andover Cottage Hospital was one of the first hundred which were built over the next 20 years, despite the negative attitude of the Andover Town Council. The term 'cottage hospital' means that the hospital did not have resident medical staff, just a nurse or superintendent, neither of whom were paid in the early stages. These hospitals were not free; everybody was expected to pay for their bed and possibly medical treatment.

Acknowledgements

My thanks are due to Andover Library, Hampshire Record Office, Winchester Reference Library, Diana Coldicott and Carol Jackson.

Andover Cottage Hospital, before 1905.

1. The First Twenty Years 1874-1894

In 1874, the Vicar of Andover, the Revd. H. B. Bousfield, suggested that Andover needed a hospital and recommended that the Pest House be converted into a proper hospital.[1] However, the Town Council saw no need for such an amenity and voted the proposal down by 7-3.

But there was a real need for a hospital and in August 1875 a scheme was mooted at the annual Venison (or Buck) Feast when the first gifts towards the hospital fund were announced.[2] Mr. William Gue, a retired Andover builder, bought a site on the eastern side of Junction road opposite the Andover Union for £1,500, Sir Charles Pressley KCB gave £1,000 for the building fund and Mr. Henry Thompson gave £500. The architect was William White FSA who estimated that the annual running costs would be about £400 pa.[3]

The formal indenture to found the hospital was dated 29 November 1875, the trustees being John Smith, John Loxley, Charles Pain and Robert Dowling. In December a public meeting was held to explain the purpose of the scheme and the chairman, George Clark, Mayor of Andover, proposed, "That it is expedient and desirable that a Cottage Hospital shall be erected for the poor of Andover and the several parishes comprising the Andover Union". (There were 32 parishes in the Andover Union.) The site in Junction Road was not everybody's first choice and when the architect explained his plans he said that while he disagreed with those who found the site objectionable, "he did not mean to say that had the promoters of the scheme had the choice of the whole town a better site could not be found but he considered it to be a very good position." Which meant that the architect was amongst those who disapproved of the site. The entrance would be from the north with a living room to the south and a mortuary could be added at a reasonable distance from the main building. Dr.George Vivian Poore suggested that there should be a bed on the ground floor since a man with a broken leg should not be carried upstairs, risking that a simple fracture might become compound.

The committee members were: William Gue, Henry Thompson, William Iremonger JP, Revd. J. Dixon, Revd. E. Y. Nepean (vicar of Appleshaw), Henry Compton (corn merchant), William Bracher (farmer), Revd. H. B. Bousfield (vicar of Andover) and George Clark, the Mayor of Andover. Hospital rules were drawn up and adopted, but a copy of the original Rule Book does not seem to have survived.

By May 1876, donations to the building fund amounted to £1,663 which was sufficient for work to commence. The foundation stone was laid by Mrs. John Loxley, the eldest daughter of the hospital's main benefactor, Sir Charles Pressley, and the vicar, the Revd. H. B. Bousfield cut the first piece of turf. Lunch was then served to 180 ladies and gentlemen in a large tent erected in the grounds. The builders were Messrs. Annett & Son.

The hospital was opened on 9th August 1877 and the cost of the building, including furnishings, surgical appliances and legal expenses, was £2,185. 12s. 10d. It stood on a large piece of ground laid out with shrubs and trees and the *Andover Advertiser* described the building as follows:

> Of red brick with an oversailing string-course pattern between the first and second floors and terminating at the springing of windows with white and red bricks formed in diamonds, the whole being covered with red tiles surmounted at the gables with tile ornamental crosses and red crimped ridges. The ground floor contains scullery, kitchen (fitted with Bealey's circulating hot water cylinder for the use of patients on the first floor), pantry and store room. Approached by a corridor is the Lady Superintendent's room, surgery, waiting room, WC and a very large day room; provision is made for a lift should one be required. The floors to the corridors are laid with black, red, buff and chocolate tiles in patterns; the rooms are floored with wood blocks laid in herring bone style on a bed of concrete, the whole surface is covered with a layer of asphalt to prevent the damp from rising. The first floor is approached from the corridor by a wide staircase, on the landing of which, upon a carved pedestal, stands a large timepiece the gift of J. W. Cockings. This leads to a large ward containing four beds and two smaller wards each of two beds. These are fitted with every convenience, including chain mattresses instead of spring beds. Adjoining these wards is a room for surgical operations. There are also bedrooms for the staff, together with a bath room, large linen closet, two WCs and housemaid's room. Internally the work is finished with a dado in red bricks, varnished, the walls being plastered above the whole of the woodwork which is stained and varnished. The builder was Messrs. Annett & Son with Thomas Page doing the stone-work. The architect was Mr. William White of 30a, Wimpole Street, London.

The first matron was Miss Killick and the medical officers were Dr. George Vivian Poore, Dr. W. Smith and Dr. W. Morrant Baker. Mr. Edward Clarke was honorary secretary and Mr. Thomas Richard Lavington became honorary treasurer.

The Annual Reports of the hospital covered the calendar years so the first one was for the period to 31st December 1877. Twenty-eight patients had been admitted but the hospital had to be closed for two months due to the illness of the assistant nurse, Miss Hamilton, who had scarlatina; it then had to be fumigated. Miss Egan was the first superintendent followed by Miss C L Jackson. The Cottage Hospital was not a free hospital and everybody was expected to pay something, commonly thought to be a minimum of 5/- but patients' payments were not included in the first accounts.[4] Potential patients had to be nominated by subscribers to the hospital; a subscriber who gave an annual subscription of £1. 1s. 0d. could nominate patients for admission but this was soon altered to 10/6d. pa.

It was the practice to distribute the accounts at the annual general meeting but the secretary was asked to distribute them before the meeting so they could be studied beforehand. The hospital needed an annual income of about £350 to stay afloat and for the first twenty years or so a shortage of money dominated committee business; doctors, matron and nurses acted unpaid. In desperation, the committee decided to follow the example of the County Hospital and publish a list of subscribers to show those who had paid and those who had not. The Mayor wondered whether this was entirely in the spirit of a Cottage Hospital but the committee went ahead and they also prepared a list of gentlemen who the committee thought should become subscribers to the hospital.

As noted, patients were expected to pay something towards their keep which meant that paupers were not admitted to the hospital. Their only hope was that the Workhouse Infirmary would be able to take them, which was conveniently across the road from the Cottage Hospital. However, in practical terms there was no difference between, say, an agricultural labourer earning 10/- per week and a pauper with no income. Neither could afford to pay for hospital treatment without assistance and this simple truth did not appear to be understood by the hospital's supporters. Time and time again the complaints about patients' payments not being enough, or even zero, were raised at the annual meetings without the slightest chance of resolution. The committee understood the problem only too well, as did the medical men; neither group would or could contemplate an absolute refusal to treat.

A young porter was injured on the railway line at Andover and he eventually died in hospital. His case was brought up because he had been recommended by a subscriber for hospital admission and could only pay 2/6d a week for his bed. But he was a member of a Friendly Society and the Society sent all his benefit to the hospital which deducted 10/- and gave the remainder to the porter's friends. Just what the 10/- covered was not clear; it seemed that the costs of medical attendance might have been paid out of hospital funds.

The medical officers either did not know the rules or read the annual accounts. Dr. Septimus Briggs Farr, an Andover GP, questioned the committee about the fees paid by patients. "How far did the fees charged to patients cover the costs?" he asked. The answer was that the amounts charged never covered the costs. Farr persevered, "I suppose patients are classed according to their means. By how much does the highest class cover their costs?" When told that all classes made a loss, Farr urged subscribers to bear this in mind when recommending cases since he fancied they tried to make it as easy as they could for the patients. Subscribers frequently paid the charges of the patients they recommended and this was calculated at 10/6d per week, excluding expert medical care. The hospital had several railway accident cases which strained resources and the Workhouse Infirmary had been placed at their disposal.

The number of patients admitted in 1891 was 68, the largest number yet. They were in hospital for 2,341 days, an average of 34 days per patient, which is an indication that the cases were becoming more complicated and costly. The hospital was still in debt and this worsened because of sanitation problems which closed the hospital for several weeks. The health of nurses and patients had been seriously affected and part of the endowment fund had to be sold to effect the necessary alterations.

The rules of the hospital regarding smoking were quite clear - there was to be none inside the hospital. But there were suggestions that perhaps it might be permitted at certain times. The chairman said that the battle of the pipe was being fought in all hospitals. He instanced Edinburgh which had led the way by allowing smoking between 6am and 7am and again between 6pm and 7pm but only in the accident ward, not in the medical ward or when other patients objected. The chairman, Janus-like, said he did not object to smoking in principle but in a small hospital like Andover "the smell would pervade everywhere". A cleric said they should consider the matter very carefully; he was a smoker himself but never smoked in his own house and thought that a man with a broken leg would not miss his pipe after the first two or three days. There was much discussion which ended with a vote, 5-4 in favour of smoking, with two abstentions, but the matron was given complete discretion in the matter.

1892 was the busiest year yet with 77 admissions and a building had been adapted for use as a mortuary at a cost of £33. The superintendent, Miss Worthington, had suffered from overwork and after a second break-down she tendered her resignation; the new superintendent was Miss Ada Britten from the West London Hospital. The hospital was said to be £100 in debt but the amount did not appear in the balance sheet. (This problem would crop up again because the so-called balance sheet was not a balance sheet.) The patients' payments were £159 and the secretary believed he could enforce payment by persuasion since several guarantors had not paid up. One reason for the deficit was that Miss Worthington had done her own dispensing but in her absence they had to have their drugs dispensed. Dr. Williams-Freeman suggested the employment of a paid nurse to relieve the superintendent and if they could get a probationer then her premium would cover the cost of a trained nurse.[5]

2. Midpoint - The Annual General Meeting for 1895

A large number of subscribers arrived for the Annual Meeting for 1895, an indication that trouble was brewing. The chairman and vicar of Andover, the Revd. Philip Richard Braithwaite, said he was glad to see so many present even if they only came to criticise and he was well aware that the hospital "was not managed on the best possible basis". As the meeting progressed it was clear that the first twenty years had produced some old scores which had to be settled.

The meeting started quietly enough: a Ladies' committee had been formed to collect small sums of 1/- upwards for a Samaritan Fund and Miss Britten the superintendent had left in April for a better job with Miss Botham taking her place. The hospital had admitted seventy-two patients who had been in hospital for a total of 1,643 days, an average of 23 days per patient. The year had started with a £50 debt but now there was a surplus of £5 with debts owing of £50, although whether these were owing to or by the hospital was not clear.

The fun then started with the chairman summarizing the events of the past few months. Letters had appeared in the press and various attempts made to make the hospital totally free for all. The basis for this seemed to be that if subscriptions were doubled then there would be more than adequate funds to make the hospital free but the chairman was not convinced this was a serious possibility worthy of discussion. He said, if it was possible to *guarantee* a doubling of subscriptions then of course the hospital could be made free for all but there was *no guarantee* that subscriptions, once started, would remain at that level. Experience had shown that subscriptions went down after the initial enthusiasm had worn off. If the hospital was free then the accommodation would have to be doubled from eight beds to sixteen to accommodate those who now went into the workhouse infirmary. The cost would be enormous and the annual subscriptions would need to quadruple and be maintained at that level for 20 years or more. The chairman reminded the meeting that the indenture founding the hospital required every patient to pay something, but these payments had fallen from £100 to £60 during the past few years. They had received several free patients and many others only contributed 2/6d per week; accident cases were received where the possibility of any payment was low or zero.

Captain Faber JP described the efforts that had been made to make the hospital free. The 154 circulars that had been sent out had only resulted in 20 new subscribers promising £22. 10s. 0d; while 14 old subscribers had promised an extra £15. This gave a total of £37. 10s. 0d. He had discussed patients' payments with the secretary and found that while patients had promised £60 the secretary had only collected £37. 10s. 0d. so there was a deficiency of £22. 10s. 0d.

During discussions about the accounts it emerged that what was described as a 'balance sheet' was really a 'receipts and payments account' with a note attached that it did not include outstanding liabilities of £75. The figures showed a balance in hand at the start of the year of £3 when there was a debt of £50, the explanation being that £3 was the balance at the bank and unpaid bills from last year were in this year's account. The figure of £75 was a true figure because the superintendent had the bills. Questions were asked about the wages paid to nurses and establishment charges. Francis Shaw said that if they knew the amount of the establishment charges and deducted these from the annual subscriptions then "they would know how much they had to work on". This would mean they should only fill four beds, not the eight they had been filling.

It was agreed that the meeting be adjourned until the financial position of the hospital could be established. There was an apparent deficit of £75 which needed to be confirmed and an advertisement would be placed in the *Andover Advertiser* asking those with claims to notify the secretary.

At the adjourned meeting it was said that the weekly cost of a bed was 17/- while the receipts per bed were 15/3d, a loss of 1/9d per bed per week. The total deficit of the hospital for the year was £39. The wages of the nurses were £28 and had not been included since they had been shown in the Samaritan Fund; if they were included in hospital costs then the cost per bed per week would be 20 shillings. Several patients did not pay anything towards either their keep or treatment.

The chairman admitted that the committee had considerable difficulty in preparing a proper balance sheet and recommended that a cash book and expenditure journal be kept together with a ledger with an account for each patient. Further, all goods supplied by tradesmen and others should be by written order signed by the chairman or his deputy and all accounts be paid by cheque. These recommendations, made by the committee to themselves, indicate a complete financial shambles, because in addition the committee had found further liabilities relating to 1883 and before of £49. 1s. 2d. The total liabilities at 31 December 1884 were therefore £87. 11s. 3d.

The revised accounts showed that patients' payments came to an average of 3/2d per week whereas the minimum payment was supposed to be 5 shillings. Complete confusion followed. The chairman did not think that a minimum had been fixed; the Revd. J. B. Fenwick (vicar of Abbotts Ann) said he always understood the minimum was 5 shillings per week; the chairman said that was the ordinary charge but not a minimum; William Bracher said there were no limits, maximum or minimum; George Clarke said the old rule was that a patient should pay a sum fixed by the committee and the patient's employer.[6] The chairman then spoke about the practical difficulties the committee experienced when dealing with patients' payments. To a large extent the committee were in the hands of the medical officers who often marked their cases as 'urgent' or 'accident' in which case the hospital was bound to take the patients without enquiry, leaving the hospital to get payment if they could. In many cases they got nothing and he instanced a case they had in the hospital now, where a person had fallen into a fire, which the chairman thought ought to have gone to the other side of the road, meaning to the Workhouse Infirmary. There was no prospect of receiving even a penny for her treatment and there was no means of enforcing payment; urgent cases were a complete lottery where payment was concerned.

Dr. Ernest Augustus Farr, the son of Dr. Septimus Briggs Farr, said it was an accident since the lady had fallen into the fire and there was no means of treating her at home. She was not a pauper, her husband had work and she was a case the hospital had to accept out of common humanity. He understood the Rector of Enham had undertaken to pay for her, but when asked the Rector said he could do nothing and thought the case was more suitable for the Workhouse Infirmary. The chairman said it was one case out of many others he could quote.

Francis Samuel Shaw (grocer) said there were cases where the patient ought to pay. He would mention no names but he could give details of those who had promised to pay and had not done so although they could well afford to pay because they were people in good positions. The chairman replied that the hospital had no means of enforcing payment; people in 'good positions' disowned liability altogether even when they had signed a guarantee promising to pay. The Revd. J. B. Fenwick said the cases from his neighbourhood were told they had to pay 5 shillings a week and they had always paid it somehow. Mr. J. W. Smith, the Andover solicitor, said the hospital should have a form which would guarantee payment, to which the chairman repeated his earlier comment that after patients left the hospital they disowned any document they had signed. "But surely the law will touch them" Smith suggested, "they have the same forms in the County Hospital". Henry Dowling did not think this was the right way to go about getting money. Shaw repeated his assertion that there were those who could pay: "I know of a person from a good family who was in hospital for 8 weeks and was sent out cured. In that case 10 shillings was paid whereas it should have been £2 and the person was well able to pay the difference. In another case there was a patient in for 8 weeks at 7/6d and he had never paid a farthing. Yet the gentleman was in a good position and able to pay what had been guaranteed".

To bring matters to a head, the chairman enquired whether the committee should be instructed to take legal action to recover the amounts, since they were obliged to take cases on written guarantees. "Is there any way to make them more binding?" he asked. Mr. F Hendy did not see what other guarantees they required other than the signature of the guarantor and though these guarantees were not enforced it was within the power of the committee to get the money. So the chairman repeated his question, should the committee take legal proceedings? Captain Faber, who was a magistrate, said that if the committee did that to a man earning £2 a week then he would not sign an order forcing him to pay. And so it all fizzled out; brave words had been spoken but human decency had won. Andover Cottage Hospital was for the poor and needy.

The Revd. Joseph Hasler (Baptist Minister) asked whether the amount paid for chemicals (medicines) was excessive since he saw further on in the report that contracts were to be arranged for the supply of drugs and did this imply that the committee had paid a larger amount than they ought to have done? The chairman confirmed this was so.

The meeting then turned to administration matters. To reduce costs the chairman said they proposed to take a bed out of use, although how this would force costs down was not clear. There was some difficulty over the signing of purchase orders when something was wanted immediately and neither he nor his deputy were in the hospital. All payments would be by cheque; a columnar cash book would be kept and the lady superintendent would have a petty cash account.

The meeting moved on to consider the hospital rules. The first was the district from which patients could be admitted. The present rule referred to the Andover Union (which consisted of 32 parishes) but the committee was now recommending 'the district of Andover'. Several points were made; there had been injustice by confining the area to the Union; the area should only be where subscribers came from; Ludgershall was excluded though the rector there would like to subscribe; the area should be defined as being a radius of so many miles. Eventually it was decided that the rule should read 'The Andover Union and such other parishes at the discretion of the committee'.

There was a lengthy discussion about doctors being on the committee since only the medical officer of Andover was on the committee as a matter of right. The Andover doctors appeared to want more say in hospital matters with more of them on the committee. It was pointed out that patients were neither admitted nor discharged without their consent so they had absolute authority over patients and had them under one roof which was a great convenience. The discussion was getting nowhere and it was finally agreed that the word 'acting' should be placed before Medical Officer.

Rule 13 was next which was the problem of patients' payments. The rule was, 'Every patient shall pay a weekly sum, the amount of which depending on their circumstances, shall be fixed by the committee.' Still the secretary did not produce the rule book. The Revd. J. B. Fenwick said patients should not be admitted for under 5 shillings per week; he had always thought this to be the case and he had either paid the sum himself or helped others. (Later he seemed to change his mind.) The chairman suggested that this would be hard on children who always paid less than 5/-. Solicitor Smith said the old rule was that they pay a weekly sum, dependent on circumstances, to be fixed in conjunction with their employers and the committee, which was pretty close to rule 13. Mr. F Hendy said the medical officers had sometimes filled in the form after consulting the patient and thought it unfair that there should be a maximum or a minimum. This had caused friction and hardship where the member of a friendly society received 12/6d a week and the medical officer said he could pay 7/6d, which left 5/- for his wife and family to live on.[7] Dr. E. A. Farr thought the amount should be fixed by the committee with a right of appeal. The Revd. J. B. Fenwick urged that those who could not afford 5/- should receive help. Captain Faber moved that the amount should be "5/- per week or such an amount as fixed by the House committee" and this was seconded. Fenwick moved that the amount "be less than 5/-" saying there were some in his village who could not afford 5/- and this too was seconded. Both motions were lost and the original rule stood unchanged.[8]

The recommended staffing levels were a superintendent (unpaid), a trained nurse (£25 pa), a probationer who should pay a premium to cover her training and maintenance, a cook (£15 pa) and a servant (£10 pa) who would not sleep in. A probationer, technically known as a scrubber, would be better for the patients and a better servant for the cook.

Finally, the committee considered the desirability of making the hospital free but were unanimous in suggesting that the matter be postponed for the time being. They thought the deficit of £88 should not to be brought into the account but should be liquidated by selling sufficient stock from the endowment fund. Further, the ladies' committee be asked to secure additional subscribers and greater care be taken to ensure that patients paid the whole of their fees. Mr. J. W. Smith disagreed saying that the endowment was the backbone of the hospital and should not be sold, especially since a large proportion of the fund came from two of his clients! He said that £87 was a mere bagatelle and could be raised within a month or so since a bazaar was to be held next month. It was agreed that the deficit should be placed in a suspense account.[9]

3. The Final Years - 1896-1926

The financial optimism of Mr. Smith (whose firm today is Messrs. Barker, Son and Isherwood) proved to be wholly justified. The following year, the ladies' bazaar raised £190 which was more than twice the amount of the deficit that had been shuffled into a suspense account. The ordinary expenditure for 1896 exceeded the income by £9 but this was made good with a gift of £5 from Admiral the Hon. Victor Montagu of Wherwell and £4 when the hat was passed round at a committee meeting. Miss Botham, the superintendent appointed the previous year, left and Miss Adela d'Darcy 'whose testimonials were most excellent' was appointed in her place, although she was to remain for barely six months.

The hospital could not keep their matrons or superintendents. They had had six in seven years, and the reason was not hard to find - they were unpaid. The committee reasoned that Andover Hospital was used as a stepping stone to better things but as a result the Hospital was acquiring an unpopular image in the town. So much so that from 1897 the matrons were paid a salary, starting with Miss H. Putz on a salary of £40 pa.

The hospital was not always full and a scheme was proposed to fill the beds. Broadly, a subscriber of £2. 2s. 0d. pa. would be given a 'free ticket' which he could give to anybody for a fortnight's stay in hospital, or indeed use it himself. For £5. 5s. 0d. pa. the 'free ticket' would give the holder a three-week stay in hospital. The scheme was not authorised at first because it was feared that it might become a drain on hospital funds, though a correspondent to the *Andover Advertiser* seemed to show that it would break even as well as fill beds. Later it was apparently approved.

By 1898 the hospital's finances were in good shape and remained so until it closed in 1926. Admissions were 80, who spent 1,501 days in hospital, an average of 18 days per patient. A shilling fund had been started to make some of the beds 'free' which was proving to be a valuable money spinner.

The rules for free nominations or free tickets were now altered. A nominated patient could remain in hospital for three weeks for each nomination obtained, instead of a three week maximum. (This was to help patients who were not cured after three weeks.) If there were no free beds the nomination letter had to be returned to the subscriber.

The rules for free nominations were continually altered. Single men in receipt of 'club pay' i.e. members of a Friendly Society, were not eligible but it was pointed out that some clubs paid more than others and after a time it was reduced to very little. To cater for this, the word 'good' was inserted before the words 'club pay' and the definition of 'good' was left to the committee. People in receipt of parish relief were not eligible for free nominations since it had been the wish of the founders to exclude those who could be dealt with under the Poor Laws. However, there had been a recent case which could not be dealt with in the Workhouse Infirmary because there were no specially trained attendants there, and the committee had admitted the person to the Cottage Hospital. But Dr. Farr said he had the power to engage specialist nursing for the Infirmary so the rule for the hospital was not altered.

Those on parish relief remained a problem because the constitution of the Cottage Hospital, rightly or wrongly, regarded the Workhouse Infirmary as the senior organisation and intended for paupers only. This was continually challenged especially since the 'Shilling Fund', to help the poor and needy, now had funds of £140. When the fund started the rules had excluded paupers but it was felt a change could be made and paupers should be admitted to the Cottage Hospital. Those in favour said that only one or two paupers could possibly be admitted during a year; those against pointed to the constitution and the fact that the hospital was nearly always full. The argument went on and on but finally the proposition was lost.

At the turn of the century the drainage system had to be renewed since there were no manholes and they had to be provided at each drain junction. The medical officers of the Borough began to voice considerable disquiet at the condition and site of the hospital; it will be recalled that the choice of site had not been unanimous in 1875. The medical men said that the hospital had been started when the majority of cases were domestic servants who were in need of rest due to afflictions of the legs and nursing was required until they were fit to return to work. (This may seem highly unlikely but that was said.) Nowadays, they said, there were more operations, the theatre was unsuitable, the building was overcrowded, it was badly ventilated, beds had to be rationed, the railway and river were too close, the wards were badly located, meals were served cold and so on. It was suggested that since the old building could not be altered, a new building would be necessary for 12 beds at a cost of about £1,500. The present building was said to be sound and the ground valuable so it was thought possible that the old building could be sold to meet the cost of the new.

Two years later, in 1903, a deposit account had been opened with the Capital and Counties Bank Ltd. for a new hospital and Henry Gamman, a business man, had promised a site behind the Workhouse on the other side of the road. The estimated cost of a new hospital with 12 beds had risen to £1,600 but the committee could not pursue the scheme until a suitable site had been found. Meanwhile, the Shilling Fund had been run down, because, as forecast, the 'free letter' scheme had been too successful. The committee had the power to refuse patients access to free beds but they had never taken such action; on this subject they said, "judging from the experience of the working classes and all classes, if they paid for something they appreciated it more".

Two years passed and there was no sign of Henry Gamman's site. It was at the top of the Workhouse garden and involved an exchange of land between the Guardians and Gamman; it seemed complicated and unlikely to happen and the subscribers decided to meet to discuss the purchase of a site. To encourage the faint-hearted, Walter Faber wrote to the *Andover Advertiser* on 17 February 1905 to say that if a mortgage of £1,100 was needed to construct a new hospital then he would pay one-half of the interest for five years. The meeting to discuss the purchase took place on 24 March 1905 and Dr. Williams-Freeman proposed, "That this meeting of the committee and subscribers decide to buy a site and to procure funds for the erection of a new hospital". The subscribers were not convinced by any means that a new hospital was necessary. "A fad of the doctors," somebody said. "Doctors, like others, allow their enthusiasm to outrun their caution and advocate schemes that others might not think necessary".

The vicar was in the chair and he handled things smoothly, saying that those who did not wish to go ahead with a new hospital, and he was one of them, were not committed to subscribe to it. Anybody who was against the idea need not vote against it because it did not bind them to anything. "The resolution he had to move this day did not commit him or the officers to a raging, tearing propaganda for a new hospital, but it would allow those who thought a new hospital necessary to get on with their scheme". Some subscribers said there was no need for a larger hospital and if they had one it would be difficult to find money for its maintenance. Others pointed out that the present hospital was nearly always full; Andover was growing fast and would increase again when the new buildings for the military were occupied. Surgery techniques were increasing by leaps and bounds and people could not be operated on in their own homes like they were years ago. As surgery advanced there was need for better accommodation and skilled nursing was important to recovery.

The question before the meeting was, "Could they raise £1,000 to expand the existing hospital using the same site, or could they raise £1,600 for a hospital on a new site?". Dr. Williams-Freeman was in favour of a new site because if the scheme foundered then rising land values would safeguard their investment. The Revd. Heanley said he had been involved with a similar scheme in Lincolnshire, increasing beds from 12 to 24, and in the course of time those who opposed it were those who took the greatest credit unto themselves when the enlargement had been successfully carried out (laughter).

Mr. Edmund Parsons, the hospital secretary, said he did not think the speakers had shown how they were going to get the £1,600 and a firm foundation was needed before they could proceed with any scheme. He doubted whether the present hospital could be sold for use as a private residence and yet it was being assumed that it could be sold as a private residence for £1,000. It would need a further £500 to make it suitable and a man who had £1,500 in his pocket for a private residence would not choose the hospital. The chairman (the vicar) said he did not know five persons who were honestly in favour of a new hospital and if they could get a purchaser for £1,000 for the hospital then he would give £50! The old hospital, he said, had only lost one patient last year so it could not be that bad.

The meeting felt that Gamman's scheme would come to nought and while many thought the present site totally unsuitable it was never intended that it should compete with either Salisbury or Winchester. Finally, Mr. Parsons said the cart was being put before the horse since they did not know whether the hospital could be sold. If it could not be sold then he proposed an addition to the proposal before the meeting, "or if this is found to be impossible to apply the funds to adding to or improving the present hospital" and this was carried.

In April 1905, Thomas Webb, Mayor of Andover, wrote to the *Andover Advertiser* asking the inhabitants to support a new hospital. "I make this urgent appeal to you to help the committee by your large or small subscriptions to carry out this sacred and benevolent object."

Nothing further was heard about purchasing a new site and in early 1906 tenders were issued for the enlargement of the hospital. The architect's plans submitted under the code name Aesculapius (the God of Medicine) were considered to be the best at a cost of £1,200. The committee had money in the bank plus definite promises amounting to £1,000 and they decided to proceed. There were to be male and female wards, a private ward, bathrooms on one long floor, a roomy operating theatre and improved accommodation for the nursing staff. F. Beale & Son from Andover undertook the enlargement.

The hospital was closed between June and December 1906 during the building works and temporary premises were obtained in Weyhill Road for patients. The enlarged hospital was opened on 6 December 1906 at a cost of £1,600. 1s. 0d, just covered by the building fund because a bazaar had produced £428 and that saved the day. The accommodation was then 10 beds, 1 cot, a private ward and a spare room for two more beds.

Over the years an endowment fund had built up by using legacies from Andover residents and the fund now produced about £50 pa. It comprised the following investments:

£313 3% L & SW Railway Debenture Stock
£1,030 India 3% Stock (Mrs. King)
£156 India 3% Stock (Mrs. Mosdell)
£104 India 3% Stock (Mrs. Harrison)
£78 2½% Consols (Mrs. Etwall)

The enlarged hospital was not heated at the outset and this was remedied in 1910. The private ward was proving to be very popular and the days of financial hardship were finally over. Two accounting quirks were observed in this year, the first when somebody asked why the figures for 1910 were being compared with those for 1908. The chairman explained that the figures for 1909 were 'not on all fours' with 1910 because they did not include unpaid bills which brought the reply that it made the

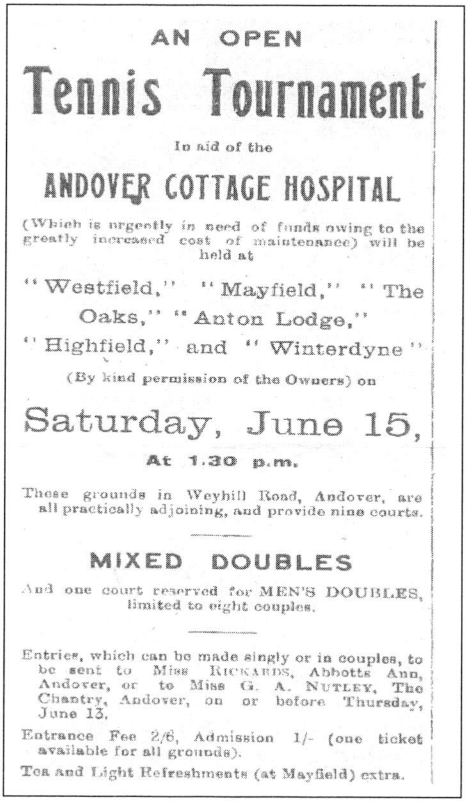

Advertisement for a Tennis Tournament in Andover, June 1918.

figures look suspicious. The second was that the accounts did not contain an amount for insurance because while the insurance cheque had been uttered it had not been presented by the insurance company and the auditors insisted that the cash book balance should agree with the bank statement.

During the war years the private ward was not as popular as in previous years since many patients chose to go to an army camp for their operations. The army authorities asked whether they could be allocated 20 beds but the committee, having only a maximum of 16 at the most, declined. An X-Ray machine was installed in 1916 at a cost of £600. By then there were 25 parishes in the union but only 12 made regular collections for the hospital.

In 1918 the rules were altered and a copy was sent to the 160 subscribers but less than 50 attended the meeting in May. A copy was sent to the Official Trustee of Charitable Funds and certain amendments had been requested all of which had been incorporated. The only outstanding item was the position of the Trustees should they wish to sell the freehold of the hospital.

In 1920 it was decided that Andover should commemorate its casualties in WWI by building a War Memorial Hospital. Over £5,000 had already been raised by private subscriptions which included £1,500 from the proceeds of a bazaar. By the following year the Memorial Hospital Fund had reached £5,608 and the secretary, Mr. Parsons, was bullish about raising finance for the new hospital, "they never had any difficulty in obtaining money to enlarge the hospital" he said.

The 1920 accounts for the Cottage Hospital showed that the gas bill had doubled and the chairman explained that the gas in the X-Ray room had to be kept going all the time. The question of insurance was raised again, because it seemed that the hospital was under-insured and at the end of the meeting the secretary doubled the cover to £4,000.

A rare tragedy occurred in December 1920 when William Alfred Hall died while under anaesthetic. At the inquest Dr. Farr was of the opinion that the deceased would not have lived had the operation not been performed but there was a chance of recovery with an operation. The jury returned a verdict that the deceased 'died of shock following haemorrhage from a gastric ulcer, probably caused by poison gas while serving in the Army.'

At Christmas 1921 the well-established Andover Debating Society discussed whether hospitals should be nationalised. Captain J. J. Saunders opened the debate by saying that everyday there were appeals for hospitals, wards were closing and staff losses, so much so he feared that the country would decline from a grade C nation to D3 or even lower. The country operated a large number of service hospitals, many poor law infirmaries and over 700 hospitals all of which were funded by the state or local authorities and Saunders urged that the nation's voluntary hospitals, like the Andover Cottage Hospital, be brought under state control. He strongly advocated one unified system instead of several overlapping systems, saying that if the whole nation contributed to a health service there could be no objection to nationalisation, *provided it did not increase the bureaucratic control under which the country was suffering.*[10] The resolution was put to the meeting and the 'noes' had nine more votes than those supporting the nationalisation motion.

Christmas was a time when the hospital was especially grateful for gifts. The *Andover Advertiser* wrote, 'the small larder and store-room will require a great deal of stuffing. The town people will be welcomed with their gifts on Thursday and those from the district on Friday and it will be advisable to be early to avoid the queues.'

A Hospital Insurance Scheme was mooted towards the end of 1922. Winchester was in the scheme as were Salisbury, Bournemouth, Reading and Oxford. The treasurer of Winchester Hospital spoke at a public meeting in Andover and related the position of Winchester before the scheme started. The hospital had been in serious financial difficulty operating with an annual deficit of £7,000 and the bankers had drawn a line under their account - enough was enough, they said. Like Andover, the problem was the need to enforce the payment of patients' charges for maintenance or ask the state to take over. Throughout the country the latter was not an acceptable option since it was felt that State control meant interference and less efficiency and greater costs. Any scheme to turn Winchester around had to accomplish two things: firstly patients *had* to pay for their maintenance in hospital (medical treatment was free); secondly, to ease the burden, patients should be given the means to pay. The answer in Winchester was to enrol men and women for a weekly subscription of 2d and the hospital would admit the subscribers without further payment. For 4d a week, a whole family would be eligible for hospital admission regardless of the number of children in the family. The necessitous poor would be admitted without any payment but those who chose not to pay the weekly sums would not be admitted free of charge, they had to pay and that would be enforced. Winchester had 20,000 members. The scheme was commended to Andover and the vote was unanimous.

By the start of 1923, the new hospital fund had reached £7,229 and it was hoped to sell the old building for £1,500. The committee decided that the funds should reach £12,500 before work commenced. The Voluntary Hospital Insurance scheme had started with 1,300 members which produced a weekly amount of £5. 8s. 4d., enough to pay the weekly maintenance costs of 11 patients, and the hospital secretary had advertised for more collectors. The hospital was well in funds but with the impending arrival of the Memorial Hospital, expenditure on the old hospital had been held back and there was a long waiting list for operations.

The committee for the new hospital proposed two wards, male and female, with 10 beds in each ward. In addition, there were to be 4 beds for children and 3 beds in a private ward, a total of 27 beds. Dr. Edwards pointed out that before the war hospitals cost £300/£400 per bed but now the figure was over £1,000 a bed. On that basis, Andover did not have nearly enough money or the prospect of obtaining it since the last quoted cost for Andover was £12,500. This discussion was getting out of hand and since the matter was in the province of the War Memorial committee and not the Cottage Hospital the chairman ruled that he was sure the financing was in good hands elsewhere.

By 1924, the Memorial Hospital Fund had reached £8,000 and the sale of the Cottage Hospital was put at £2,000, an increase of £500 from the year before. The Voluntary Insurance Scheme had now attracted 2,100 entrants, the private ward was doing well and a new boiler had been installed - it could not be delayed any longer.

The site of the new War Memorial Hospital was given by Henry Gamman who had lost both his sons in the war. He had purchased an expanse of land off the Charlton Road and gave it all to the War Memorial Committee, who were thus spared the expense of buying it. (Mr Gamman died in March 1926 shortly before the new hospital was opened.)[11]

In February 1925, Mr. Parsons gave details of the tenders received for the new hospital, the winning tender being that of Messrs. Musselwhite & Son from Basingstoke with £15,293. An overdraft facility had been obtained from Lloyds Bank for £4,000/5,000 and it was hoped that donations would provide sufficient funds so the overdraft facility would not be required. The foundation stone of the Memorial Hospital was laid by Major General Seeley, the Lord Lieutenant of the County. The Cottage Hospital had never been registered as a charity but before it could be sold, approval of the Charity Commissioners had to be obtained.

The last Annual General Meeting of Subscribers was held on 19 March 1926. The matron, Miss H. Putz, had just resigned after 30 years' service because she felt that with advancing years she could not cope with the demands of a new and larger hospital. Dr. Farr, the senior medical officer, presented her with a cheque for £100 and recalled a story told by Dr.Williams-Freeman that when Miss Putz joined the hospital the surgeons had to wait until the servants and patients had had their lunches. Only then could they use the table for operating purposes!

On June 26th the patients from the Cottage Hospital were moved into the Memorial Hospital which was opened officially on June 30th by Field Marshal the Viscount Allenby. Kenneth Down from Charlton School presented the Field Marshal with a cheque for hospital funds. The Memorial Hospital started with 24 beds and could be extended if necessary. The total cost was £16,500; £13,000 had been collected already and the Hampshire County Council was expected to buy the Cottage Hospital for £2,000. That left £1,500 which had been promised by wealthy donors.

Andover Cottage Hospital had been open for 48 full years between 1878 and 1925. During that time 5,202 patients were admitted for treatment and most of them were cured and discharged. Over the years there had been a general increase in the number of patients admitted; in the final year hospital usage was 89%. The average length of time that patients spent in the hospital varied over the years from 23 days in 1894 to 13 days in 1924; the average over the whole period was 19 days. Clearly the hospital had met a real need in the Andover area during the years it was open.

The opening of the Andover War Memorial Hospital, 1926. (HPP34/073)

Notes:

1. John Spaul. *Andover 950-1974.* (2004) p.144.
2. This is still celebrated in many parts of mainland Europe when the flesh of wild animals is eaten between mid-October and mid-January.
3. William White (1825-1900) was one of the High Victorian Gothic architects who had trained under Giles Gilbert Scott. The church of St. Michael, Lyndhurst (completed in 1870) is considered to be his greatest work.
4. This point cropped up again and again. Nobody seemed to know what the minimum was, or indeed if there was one.
5. It was estimated that the cost of training a nurse was at least £50 which limited the intake to the middle classes.

6. Rule 13 in the Hospital Rule Book was at best ambiguous. 'Every patient shall pay a weekly sum, the amount of which depending on their circumstances, shall be fixed by the committee'. The secretary, perhaps wisely, did not produce his Rule Book which was surely in the drawer of the desk where he was sitting. This would only have added to the confusion since the rule allowed for as many interpretations as there were committee members.
7. In Victorian times the majority of working men made a small weekly payment to a local Friendly Society which acted as a benefit club in times of sickness and death.
8. Admissions to the Pest House for infectious diseases were made on the understanding that patients had to pay their costs, but perhaps the Pest House secretary also had difficulty in collecting the dues.
9. A popular way of dealing with an embarrassment. It will not go away but is not a constant reminder of something that we wish had not happened.
10. The italics are the author's.
11. David J. Borrett. 'Henry Gamman. Entrepreneur and local benefactor' in *Lookback at Andover. 2005.* vol.2 no.6, pp.189-197.

ANDOVER AND NEW STREET IN THE GREAT WAR
1914-1918

Harry W. Paris

The photographs that have been used to illustrate this article are all from the Harry Paris Collection; those that appear with reference numbers are now part of the Hampshire Photographic Project.
At the time of the Great War the Guildhall was known as the Town Hall; the Corn Exchange was at its ground level. Abbreviations used are noted at the end.

The date of 4th August 1914 dawned bright and clear. Many of the Newstreeters realised the significance of the news that Austria had declared war on Serbia. Those who were fortunate enough to have attended Tidworth Tattoo during the previous week were thrilled by the display, little realising that those taking part would soon be called upon to carry out more serious duties. Indeed, already the Salisbury Plain Rifle Club had called off their shoot as their military members, together with certain Territorial Army detachments, had been called upon to man vital coast defences. And the organisers of the Flower Show to be held on the Walled Meadow found themselves without a band or competitors for the Military Sports they had arranged.

Saturday and Sunday had seen the arrival of many TA units at Ludgershall for their annual camp who, led by their bands, had marched away to the Windmill Hill camp. But as their regular army officers had been called back to their regiments and no army instructors were available, these TA units were sent back to their depots to await developments.

New Street was agog with the news that war with Germany was possible. One party living at the top of the street refused to cancel their Bank Holiday trip and they travelled to Southampton to give the children their first glimpse of the sea. Arriving at Southampton West Railway Station, they went over the level crossing onto the beach which at that time extended unbroken to the pier head. Making their way along the beach they eventually arrived at the pier head and boarded a paddle steamer *en route* for Cowes and Ryde. The realisation that things were not as they appeared to be came when out of Portsmouth harbour steamed heavy units of the Navy on their way to take up their war stations. This realisation was confirmed when they arrived at the West Station and found the platforms crowded with reservists awaiting trains to convey them to their units. After a long wait the parents managed to carry the children on to a train and keep them awake long enough to see the lights of the yachts on Southampton Water.

With the arrival of the papers on Tuesday morning came the news that England was at war with Germany and the realisation that those men in New Street who were Army Reservists or members of the TA would be called to the colours to join the 300,000 men who comprised the British Army, which was the smallest in Europe – referred to by the Kaiser as England's 'Contemptible Little Army'.

Wessex Division of the Territorial Army outside the Drill Hall, 1914. (HPP34/083)

That morning two of the boys who had been on the trip the day before were out in the street gathering horse manure in the buckets they had played with on the beach when they saw Mr Horne, whom they both knew very well, coming towards them. He was dressed in Army uniform, complete with his equipment, on his way to the Drill Hall in East Street where the local company of the ASC Wessex Division TA were mustering. The boys watched as the men were issued with their rifles and filled their bandoliers with live ammunition. The transport column later marched away to entrain for Aldershot while those remaining marched to Bulford, leaving behind them many anxious wives and mothers.

The evening papers were in great demand as people eagerly searched for news. (Newspapers cost a halfpenny.) Local tradesmen financed a telegram service which posted the latest news in the Bridge Street Post Office.

The next day it was the turn of the Yeomanry to muster. This they did with their horses in a field off Charlton Road. They were joined by the farmers of the district with their cart horses from their farms. Army vets were in attendance and all the horses passing their examination were purchased for the Services. Two horses named Johnny and Darling from New Street Farm were not acceptable as being too young.

Two of the busiest places in Andover at this time were the railway stations as train after train passed through carrying the assembling BEF. Crowds of well-wishers lined the level crossing to cheer the troops waving from the windows of the trains conveying them to France to confront the mighty German Army.

After the departure of the BEF to the tune of 'Tipperary', Andover settled down to a wartime footing. There was a great demand for labour as hutted camps were being built across Salisbury Plain. With the advent of the camps there was a big demand for catering contractors. One of these was W. G. Young of High Street, Andover. With a number of Tilling & Stevens Petrol Electric Lorries, he operated all over the Plain and Newbury race course. He provided the Newstreeters with a job which made those who participated weep. A wagon driven by Mr Eastman entered the street and delivered to certain houses a sack of onions. The occupants were contracted to peel these ready to be pickled, when they would be collected. The weather being warm, the work was carried on outdoors so the whole street smelled of onions, even the schools being affected. The schoolmasters could do nothing about it. They just had to grin, or in this case weep, and bear it.

In a hamlet called Cutty, consisting of six houses and a pub, there was a factory owned by a firm named Kynopes who produced gunpowder. They drew a lot of their workers from a nearby village, Longparish, but in response to an appeal for labour a group of women from New Street went to work there, walking the four miles each way. Taskers later employed women in the making of shells.

Munitions workers from Cutty, 1914.

Meanwhile a new army was being recruited, named after a well known British General whose picture pointing with his index finger over the inscription 'Your Country Needs You' was to be seen throughout the country. Named 'Kitchener's Army', they wore whatever uniforms were available, some blue and some khaki, some with forage caps, others with peak caps. Tidworth Barracks, Perham Down and Bulford Camp became their parade grounds, while thousands were camped on Windmill Hill and Tidworth Fields.

The personal equipment issued to a private soldier was: 3 pairs socks, 2 shirts, 2 pairs pants, 2 towels, woollen sleeping cap, 1 cardigan jacket, 1 razor, 1 housewife [a pocket case for needles and thread etc], shaving brush, hair brush, knife, fork, spoon and mug. The allowance paid to servicemen's wives was: wife 12s 6d; 1 child 15s 0d; 2 children 17s 6d; 3 children 20s 0d; 4 children 22s 0d; each extra child 2s 0d. In the event of a soldier dying, his wife's pension was: widow with 4 children £1; widow with 3 children 17s 6d; widow with 2 children 15s 0d; widow with 1 child 12s 6d; widow with no children 7s 6d.

An army of workmen were building huts on Perham Down to house the colonials who were sailing in from all parts of the Empire. I remember travelling with my mother on a wagonette drawn by two horses for a Sunday afternoon ride taking in Weyhill, Perham Down and Ludgershall. We saw one New Street man working on the huts, a carpenter named Sammy Steele.

Early in October the 4th TA Battalion Hampshire Regiment, which included many Andover men, sailed to India to replace the regular battalion.

Andover at weekends became a hive of soldiers who had come in from the various camps. The Corn Exchange was used as a canteen which, supported by voluntary contributions and workers, provided facilities for writing, reading and hot drinks. It was known a the Soldiers' Rest.

Arriving in Andover in October 1914 were the Belgian war refugees who were housed in Clare House in East Street. They were financed by voluntary contributions from various charities and local associations. New Street Mission Room and Sunday School promised a shilling a week.

Early in November the troops began to move out of Tidworth Barracks into billets in the villages. The barracks were taken over by Canadian troops. As the weather and conditions in the tented camps deteriorated, a billeting survey was made of Andover. Men were billeted four to a room and were issued with two blankets and slept on the floor.

It was a very apprehensive Andover that awaited the arrival of the units of Kitchener's Army from 'Perishing Down'. The troops left their wet, cold and muddy

Soldiers parading in front of the Globe Inn, Andover.
(HPP34/231)

The 7th Battalion of the Leicestershire Regiment marching down Upper High Street after a church parade.
(HPP34/006)

camps to march to Andover and warm, dry billets. Down the Weyhill Road they came, all 3000 of them in their motley uniforms, packs upon their backs, with rifles slung across their shoulders or carried at the trail, singing popular and regimental songs until they reached the Round House when the order came 'March to attention'. Each battalion ceased their singing, straightened their packs and caps, sloped arms and with head held high, led by their band and a mounted officer, marched into Andover to be welcomed by the Andoverians.

Andover with its population of 8000 had become an armed camp. The troops were billeted all over the town, with the three main training area being the Recreation Ground, a meadow in South Street, and the grounds of Croye House serving those who were billeted in New Town. Mr Henry Gamman lived in Croye House and owned the meadow in South Street, both of which he volunteered. The fee paid for the billets was 2s 6d with board and others in proportion. A cookhouse had been erected in the acre opposite the Borough Arms, the Drill Hall serving as a mess room. A rifle range situated in the Daisy Dell off the Ladies' Walk, normally operated by the Andover Rifle Club, was much in use.

From early morning onwards the Andover streets rang to the tramp of iron shod feet as the troops trained for the grim trials that awaited them. Without a pass they were not allowed in the streets after 9.00 pm, and patrols ensured that this order was carried out. Saturday evening was generally spent preparing for church parade on Sunday morning. Buttons, badges and boots had to shine. Seven hundred and fifty marched up the High Street to St Mary's Church where the services were conducted by their chaplains. After the service they formed in fours behind their bands and marched down the High Street, each company striving to appear the smartest. They certainly impressed the people of Andover who lined the streets. Services for the Roman Catholics were held in the old Post Office in the High Street. Other denominations were welcomed into the various chapel congregations in the town.

Organisations in the town provided entertainments, the Town Hall and the Assembly Rooms being in great demand. Andover Football Club played several matches with the regimental teams, also incorporating the troops in their own teams. The constant training was beginning to tell on the Recreation Ground - hardly a blade of grass was to be seen.

Among the main items of the troops' training were the route marches. As their physical condition improved, so did the length of these marches increase until a 12 mile one on the dusty or muddy roads proved to be quite a test of their stamina. Round the district, companies of troops could be seen swinging along carefully watched by their NCOs who, whenever the pace flagged, encouraged them to sing. Not everyone would have recognised the words they adapted to well known tunes but the boys who often accompanied them on their marches quickly learnt the words, indeed they introduced words of their own. One of the favourites was 'Fred Karno's Army' and standing in the Rec. and hearing their instructors' comments one might have agreed with their own assessments. But there was a deadly seriousness about their training that was impressive.

The Church Army in the form of Captain Clare and his wife, who were conducting an evangelical tour of the Winchester diocese in a Church Army caravan, extended their stay in the New Town area to serve the troops in that district. Operating from the Millway Road Mission Room with voluntary workers, they conducted services and organised entertainments, reading and writing facilities being made available. The Newstreeters played their part, many of their guests attending the lively services peculiar to the Mission Room and joining in the hymn singing so dear to the congregation. Other events were staged on their behalf, not forgetting the darts matches in the pubs.

As the weeks went by the improvement in the troops' military efficiency and physical standard showed in their bearing, which was helped by the replacement of motley uniforms with the standard khaki.

During this period spy scares were being started all over the country and Andover was no exception. A general shop in New Street was kept by a man named Arthur E. Shenton who was altogether different from his neighbours. A dapper little man in white apron and coat, plus a moustache which matched the Kaiser's and a military bearing, somehow became an object of suspicion. He went to London and underwent an examination. As a result he was given a certificate to be placed in the shop window announcing his loyalty to the Allied cause. He was referred to after this event as 'German Shenton'. He left Andover shortly afterwards and his shop was taken over by Edwards & Barnards as a branch of their shop in Winchester Street, under the management of Mr Cheeseman.

Six weeks after entering Andover the Lancashire Brigade, now as 'fit as fiddles', their morale high, fully uniformed, with their equipment complete, paraded in Andover for the last time and marched up the Weyhill Road en route for Tidworth. Quite a number of boys accompanied them as far as the Hundred Acre Corner, where they stopped and waved their friends goodbye as they watched them go down the hill on their way to the bloody battlefields of France where so many would end their earthly journey, but never would they forget the Christmas they spent among the Andoverians. They spent six weeks in Clevedon before going to France to take up their place as the 56th Infantry Brigade of the 2nd Army.

Albert Stockwell, generally known as 'Spesh', living in Bartletts Buildings in New Street, father of one of New Street's well known families, received a letter from the King's Keeper signed by the Privy seal appreciating the fact that he had five sons serving in the Army. The names of the sons were Albert and Vince, 21st Lancers; Charles, Trooper 1st Dragoon Guards; Harry and Archie, Army Service Corps.

In the early days of the Great War the boys of the New Street School were taught two colonial songs, both appreciated by colonial troops. The songs were as follows:

Rally round the banner of your country,
Take the field with brothers over the foam
On land, see wherever you may keep your eye on Germany,
For England, home and beauty have no cause to fear,
Australia will be there
Australia will be there.

In days of yore from Britain's shore
Wolfe the dauntless hero came and planted firm Britannia's flag
On Canada's fair domain.
There now it flies our boast and pride
The maple leaf for ever.
God save our king and heaven bless
The maple leaf for ever.

As the young men left to join the services labour became scarce, with demand in the Andover district increased owing to the military activities. Consequently wages were rising rapidly. This caused discontent among the agriculture workers and, getting little or no satisfaction from their employers, they began to change their employment. One woman complained to the *Andover Advertiser* that people were being paid 23 shillings to billet one soldier for a week, while she had to clothe and feed a family of six on her husband's wages of 13 shillings a week. She quoted her weekly budget: coal 1s 9d, 3d for a faggot of wood, 5d for a gallon of paraffin, 3d club subscription, 4d insurance, 2 shillings rent, making a total 5 shillings and leaving 8 shillings to feed and clothe six. To maintain their labour force the farmers were obliged to raise their employees' wages.

Previous to Christmas 1914, parcels of goodies were sent to the Andover men serving in France. In their letter of thanks, Rifleman I. Butler and Rifleman Clark of B Company 3rd Rifle Brigade described how they spent their Christmas day. They were in their trenches, 200 yards from the Germans. They joined in the carols which they heard the Germans singing. After a while they observed the Germans coming out of their trenches, unarmed, and still singing. They joined them in No Man's Land where, surrounded by the stinking bodies of their dead comrades, they exchanged gifts of cigarettes and sweets in a peculiar atmosphere. The officers arranged a truce to enable the dead to be buried, after which they returned to their trenches and listened to a German band playing in their trenches. Hostilities were resumed the next morning.

After the Lancashire Brigade departed, leaving behind them in the training areas all the paraphernalia of war, Andover was comparatively quiet, although the Town Hall was still in great demand as the troops sought relaxation from their training in the Perham and Tidworth area – not forgetting a plate of bread and butter and a cup of tea for 2½d plus writing materials free. This quiet did not last long as the billets were occupied by the 10th Battalion City of London Royal Fusiliers, known as the Gilded Tenth, and the 7th Battalion Leicestershire Regiment. The Royal Fusiliers had an excellent band which gave several concerts in the Assembly Rooms and headed the church parades. The Leicestershire Regiment gave the town a fine military bearing as they beat the retreat outside the Town Hall every evening.

The constant military traffic, guns with their iron tyres, motor lorries with solid rubber tyres, beside the scuff of the horses' shoes and the constant tramp of the infantry, was placing a terrific strain on the roads. Vigo Road in particular was four inches deep in mud at one time and having to be swept by a horse drawn sweeping appliance. New Street received the same treatment but had the addition of manure as the cows from New Street Farm wended their way through the gate adjoining the cuckoo pen (as the fenced in walk way ending in a kissing gate was called) into Farm Close and down the street to the water meadows in the Watery Lane area. As the weather improved, the mud turned to dust which had to be laid by horse drawn water carts which consisted of a large tank mounted on four wheels and sprayed on the road from the rear, much to the delight of the children as they pushed one another into the spray.

New Street became a main thoroughfare for the motor lorries carrying rations and equipment to the troops in Tidworth, Perham Down and Bulford areas, as well as the tented camps. The children became quite expert in recognising the different makes of lorries, including Commer Cars, Dennis, Leyland, Thornycroft and Maudsley. They all bore the insignia of the War Department and were subject to a speed limit of 30 mph.

As the schools were overcrowded, certain classes functioned in the local chapel classrooms. My particular classroom was situated in the chapel in Bridge Street. The town river flowed alongside and our playground was cantilevered over the river and the roadway leading to the Town Mill. The horse drawn batteries of the Royal Field Artillery on their way to the ranges at Larkhill used Bridge Street as a resting place. When the boys came out to play they often found the batteries drawn up along the street and the horses being watered in the river. Each gun and ammunition limber being drawn by six horses meant the river was very crowded. The boys were thrilled to see so many wonderful horses, little realising what terrible suffering they later would be called upon to bear.

Later, after considerable activity in a meadow behind New Street Farm, enquiries by the boys revealed that Andover was to be the overnight stopping place for the 60lbs guns of the Royal Artillery. The guns were to be parked in the High Street and the horses were to be accommodated in the horse lines being prepared at New Street. When the guns arrived the boys formed a reception committee. They found the sight of the big guns, each hauled by 12 heavy horses, overwhelming as they followed

A 60lbs gun.

the horses to New Street Farm. A pantechnicon served as a guardroom and the boys accompanied the soldiers as they patrolled the horse lines. Some of the boys would get up early in the morning to see the horses and the guns on their hilly way to Larkhill and the hell that awaited them beyond. What did it matter if they were late for school and collected two strokes with the cane?

The boys thought they had seen the biggest of the guns but following the 60lbs guns came the 9.2 Howitzers hauled by a Holt tractor. Guns and tractors were all parked in the High Street and the men billeted in public houses. The boys were fascinated by the tractors but you could not stroke their noses and they were not interested in an apple core or a crust of bread – and they did stink of paraffin and petrol.

Later came the Pack Artillery, another type of gun and another animal. The guns were carried on the backs of mules. They did not march but walked at the mules' pace. The guns had to be loaded on the mules very correctly or sores would appear and the animals would become very uncooperative. They used to camp on the Sheep Fair in London Road. What a difference to the big guns. They would come walking up London Street towards the Sheep Fair and then were away in the morning to be seen no more.

*

With the coming of conscription a new body came into being, known as the Borough Tribunal. This was formed from local dignitaries together with a military officer who stated the case for the Army very firmly. Members of the tribunal, to prevent them being brought under pressure from relatives, friends and employers, were not informed of the identity of the appellant before he was brought before them. It was a very serious business. They considered appeals against conscription on religious grounds, dependents, hardships, vital employment etc. Exemptions were granted for periods, at the expiry of which a further appeal could be made.

At one period of the war men who had their appeal rejected could be listed as 'Killed in Action' eight weeks later. Men in essential employment or reserved occupations were subject at times to insulting remarks from the public and became the recipient of a white feather. Under a system known as Lord Derby's Scheme they were given an arm band inscribed 'War Service'. Men working in essential government departments were liable to be conscripted and then after receiving basic military training were returned to their original employment, becoming subject to military discipline and rates of pay. The need for soldiers was so great that men could be working at their jobs, receive their calling up papers and then after six weeks training were reported 'Killed in Action'.

The 7th Battalion Leicestershires were responsible for a 'battlefield' which they created near the Plantation at the top of Old Winton Road. They dug a complete system of trenches, complete with firing bays, dugouts and barbed wire. This area was continually in use, day and night. Barbed wire fences were erected in the dark and there were bayonet charges in and out of the trenches – altogether a place to be given a wide berth by the faint hearted.

Andover Advertiser. May 1916. Andover Hospital Supply Depot. 'Under the auspices of the British Red Cross, a depot has been formed to be known as the Andover Hospital Supply Depot. Its object is to make and supply hospitals with bandages, swabs and hospital garments. It is situated with kind permission of Mr Percival Clarke over his business premises in Bridge Street. Miss Dugey has furnished the room. Volunteers are required to help with the project in various forms. Mrs Richard and Mrs Berkley will be responsible for the organisation of the project.'

Meanwhile, Australian soldiers were convalescent at Rothsay Hospital, having arrived there via the Dardanelles, Egypt and France prior to another tour of active service.

Some of the old boys of New Street, whilst on leave from their units, came to the school and gave the scholars an account of their experiences. One was a pilot in the Royal Flying Corps whose talk proved to be of particular interest.

*

A new theatre of war came to the notice of the Andoverians when it was learned that a number of local men who had been serving in India were part of the Anglo-Indian Expeditionary Force campaigning in Mesopotamia. They were opposing the Turkish drive on the Persian Gulf and India. They were successful under General Townsend until they captured Kut al Mara, 346 miles from the Persian Gulf. They were desperately in need of reinforcements. A third of their forces had to be returned to India suffering from dysentery and malaria. The main supply lines were the two rivers, the Euphrates and the Tigris. Eventually the main army had to retreat, leaving the garrison of Kut al Mara besieged by the Turkish Army. The siege lasted from 15 December 1915 until 29 April 1916 when, with no medicines, supplies or food, they surrendered. Altogether 5746 men died during the siege or the following captivity. In March 1918 news was received of the men of Kut who were prisoners in Ada Barcar near Constantinople, the first since November 1915. Col. W. Faber ascertained the names of the 5th Hants Battery RFA who were prisoners. A New Street man, one of Buffer Rolfe's sons, survived the siege and returned from captivity in 1918.

During the summer of 1916 the Clatford Rec. was pressed into service, this time as a cricket field when both the Andover Cricket Club and the Clatford Cricket Club played the Australian troops at cricket, with little success.

June 2nd 1916. A Russian Flag Day was held in Andover to raise funds to support a bed in a hospital in Petrograd.

A Flag Day on the High Street, Andover, 1917.
(HPP34/020)

The military had taken over every building used for public assembly except churches and schools. Early in December 1916 the Durham Light Infantry arrived to take over the billets. Cookhouses were built in various parts of the town to cope with the food for the soldiers, as civilians were finding it difficult to find extra food. Having impressed the locals with their military bearing and their band's musical ability, the DLI left after a three months training stint. Their place was taken by Canadian troops. As labour on the farms was in short supply, soldiers were detailed to help with the harvest.

Andover was very popular with the colonial troops in the district, the Australians being particularly attracted to New Street where they were made very welcome. They found the atmosphere more to their liking than the more sedate parts of the town. With four pubs to choose from, they created very jovial and gay evenings with little thought for tomorrow. They were very popular with the boys and this led to trouble for one of them.

Harry Smith, aged 9 years, commonly known as Dicky, was a problem. He ran away from home and joined up with the Australians on Perham Down. They fitted him out with a miniature uniform complete with a bush hat and adopted him as their mascot. The school inspector reported the matter to the police who collected young Dicky, much to his disgust, and returned him to his parents together with a summons to appear before the court to account for his absence from school. His mother, a very small woman, pleaded that she had to work as a washerwoman at the Anton Laundry to help feed her family. She was warned regarding Dicky's school attendance. The young man himself was given a good talking to by the magistrates and threatened with a spell in a reform school if he again transgressed.

For a time Dicky's school attendance was normal until one evening during harvest time he was entrusted with a wagon and horse from New Street Farm to bring in a load of corn from the harvest field. He conned three boys, Joe Hardy and his brother 'Beano' and Harry Paris, with the story that the corn was to be gathered at Charlton. Instead, with Dicky driving, they found themselves approaching Perham Down. Meanwhile the police had been informed, who in turn warned the military what was likely to happen. When the culprits arrived the Australian Military Police turned them straight round and sent them back to Andover. As they approached the Railway Tavern in Weyhill Road the three passengers deserted the wagon, leaving Dicky to drive down the Weyhill Road into the arms of the police. As a result of this escapade and a similar one with a horse and trap, he left his Australian friends and spent his remaining boyhood days in a reform school.

The Canadians were the next to be billeted in Andover.

*

Andover had had early contacts with flying. Pilots flying from Farnborough to Salisbury Plain made Andover their turning point and in consequence a number of forced landings took place in the vicinity. When the airfield at Larkhill was developed as a flying school by the Royal Flying Corps, aeroplanes were often to be seen in the air over Andover. The hazards of flying had been brought home to the locals when an Andover man, Staff Sgt. Richard Wilson, was killed in an air crash near Stonehenge in 1912. His body had been taken to his parents' home in Andover and he was given a full military funeral and burial in Andover churchyard. His grave was marked by a cross bearing a marble model of a plane; later the blades of the propeller were broken by vandals.

In 1916 the town was thrilled to hear that the RFC were coming to take over an aerodrome being developed on a site in the Weyhill Road, one and a half miles out of Andover, known locally as Hundred Acres Corner. The trees each side of the road leading to Monxton were cleared and a camp site including hangars was being built. The first hangars were metal framed covered with canvas. Later three brick structures with wooden roofs covered with felt were built. German prisoners were employed in making the roads. The Hundred Acre field made an ideal landing ground. One particular landmark which disappeared was a copse at the junction of the Weyhill and Monxton roads, well known to shepherds driving their sheep to Weyhill Fair as it marked the halfway stage to Weyhill from Andover.

Aerial view of Andover Airfield, 1918.

The Royal Flying Corps uniform of khaki, forage caps, double breasted tunics, britches and putties made yet another addition to the variety of uniforms to be seen in Andover, and yet another badge to be worn on the collector's belt.

During the summer on Sunday afternoons hundreds of people could be seen making their way up the Weyhill Road to watch the flying. The noise of the aircraft engines, mixed with the sound of the guns firing on the Larkhill ranges, brought the sound of war very near. The RFC tenders bearing the Crossley Badge on their radiators joined the other military traffic in the district.

Following the increase in flying there came a number of fatal accidents. As the airfield was situated in the parish of Penton, the victims were buried in Penton churchyard, the burial service being conducted by the parish priest, Rev. Badger, who was chaplain of the RFC camp. The area in the churchyard where the men were buied came to be known as 'The Airmen's Corner'. The collection of souvenirs from wrecks became all the vogue among the boys, particularly the elastic which provided the spring in the aircrafts' landing gear.

*

German submarine warfare was causing serious food shortages. A local food committee was set up to be responsible for the distribution of available food to retailers, their quota being determined by the number of customers registered with them. It was still a matter of luck if you were there when the food arrived. It was difficult for mothers who had to go to work. Children would stand in the queue for any food that was going.

Millers were allowed to include 7lbs of potato flour in every bag of wheat flour. Bakers were not allowed to sell bread until it had been baked at least 12 hours. It was called 'Standard Bread'. Human nature being what it is, it was not surprising that certain tradesmen took advantage of the conditions and raised the price of commodities in short supply. They were referred to as war profiteers. To avoid the necessity for children to take sandwiches to school, a canteen was opened in the Drill Hall. A midday meal was provided for children under 15 years for 3d and under 10 years for 2d. An average of 300 children a day took advantage of this offer.

An advertisement appeared in the *Andover Advertiser* inviting the public to gather blackberries, to be made into jam, and deliver them to centres sited in local schools. If the weather was warm and dry the children returning to school after their midday break would see in the playground a blackboard with the words 'Blackberry Holiday' written upon it. This was the signal for a mad scamper to dash home and get their containers and away to Cowdown Copse, Harewood Forest, Bell Grove or wherever the fruit was to be found. The New Street children were very keen as, apart from helping the war effort, they received 3d a pound for all fruit delivered to the school.

On Fridays the fruit from the local schools was brought into the town by carrier carts and delivered to New Street School. The school porch contained the New Street consignment whilst outside stood consignments from the National School and the lots from Hurstbourne Tarrant, Charlton, Penton, Kimpton, Abbotts Ann, Amport, Upper Clatford, Tangley, Vernham Dean, Upton, Ashmansworth and Nether Wallop schools, all ready to go to the Junction Station to be dispatched to London. Altogether parents and children collected 10 tons 3½ lbs of fruit and received £280-3s-4½d. They were all weighed on the school scales in quantities ranging from ½ lb to ½ cwt. Tiny tots received 1½d. The town schools collected 5tons 3cwt 9½lbs. They also collected horse chestnuts (conkers) for the gunpowder factory near Longparish.

*

Between 1914 and 1918, 6452 troop trains and 1485 ambulance trains passed over the Midland and South West Junction Railway, which included Andover, Tidworth and Ludgershall.

One Sunday afternoon late in 1916 two boys, after attending New Street Sunday School, went for a walk to the Junction Station [the present Andover Station] to watch the troop trains passing through. They were about to go home when they realised that the London train was shortly due. They went on to No.2 platform and standing on one side they watched the would be passengers and their relatives and friends making their way down the subway and on to No.3 platform to await the arrival of the train. Among the groups were a number of leave expired soldiers returning to their units, some with their buttons, badges and brasses brightly polished and carrying a swagger stick, mostly accompanied by a smiling girl.

About half a dozen soldiers were in a different category. All their badges were cloth and the buttons dull. They also wore a divisional emblem. Their uniforms, obviously having been recently washed and pressed, showed signs of hard wear. These men, seven days previously, had come from the trenches of northern France. The relatives and friends who accompanied them were very subdued, the wives and girl friends under a great strain as they smiled and held back the tears. Someone tried to start a song when a signal announced that a train would be pulling into No.4 platform. A hush came over the people as they realised that this was a hospital train carrying wounded men from France.

The long white train, emblazoned at intervals along its long length with large red crosses, was a symbol of hope for relief from pain and suffering. The smiling eyes in the grey faces of the wounded, some of them little more than boys, brought tears of sorrow and anxiety to the eyes of those present whose loved ones in less than 48 hours would be facing the same terrible dangers.

The whole station grew very quiet as some of the stretchers containing the wounded were placed on the platform, some minus one or more limbs or an eye, others with no apparent injury but for whom life would never be the same as it had been before they had been called to the colours just eight weeks earlier. Then, a brave, fit young man; now brave but a pitiful wreck – the debris of war, but still someone's loved one. The train with its precious contingent and their nurses pulled out of the station. Ambulances were waiting in the road beyond the railway lines. The stretchers were carried across and the wounded were sent on the last stage of their journey home from that 'stinking, muddy and bloody jungle beyond the barbed wire' where man hunted man. Some were never to parade in uniform again. Others, after an all too brief respite, were to return to the gates of hell with a gold stripe on their left sleeve to tell the world that they had manned the breach and suffered.

The London train was signalled and drew into the platform. All was bustle as last farewells were said. The soldiers, carrying their rifle and accoutrements and bound for 'somewhere in France', boarded the train awkwardly followed by other passengers. Having dumped their belongings they leaned from the carriage windows to hold the hands and look into the damp smiling faces of their loved ones. The porter shouted "Stand away from the doors". A last hurried embrace. The green flag waved and the train slowly moved away from a very quiet station.

*

24 May 1916.

Early in May people passing the Council Boys School on a Friday afternoon noticed that the songs the boys were singing had a distinctive martial air. This also applied to the girls during their singing lesson. Also, it was noticeable that in place of the customary static physical drill by individual groups, they were parading and marching round the playground. At times the whole school would take part. In their turn, the girls were doing the same. Had you enquired the reason for this particular activity, you would have been told that they were preparing for Empire Day. During their play time the children could be heard singing the following ditty:

Twenty fourth of May
Is Empire Day.
If they don't give us a holiday
We will all run away.

Came the day. The children came to school dressed for the occasion, the girls in white pinafores and gay ribbons in their hair, the boys with shining boots and their hair plastered down with water. After assembly and the marking of the register, Mr Daniels and Miss Webb went into the playground to greet the Mayor, Mr F. W. Bingham, and the Mayoress. He was supported by Mr McLoughlin, the Misses Beale and the Misses Bracher, the Vicar, Rev. W. Smith, and Rev. Lucas. Two boys

Boys of New Street School with Mr. Daniels, c.1919. (HPP34/145)

approached the flagpole which stood in the centre of the railings which divided the boys' and the girls' playgrounds. This was the signal for the scholars to assemble. In their turn, the boys and girls marched past the saluting base at the foot of the flagpole and took up their allotted places. Mr Noble conducted the singing of the verses of the National Anthem.

After a prayer by the vicar the Mayor addressed the children. He spoke of the history of the glorious British Empire on which the sun never sets. He stated how at Britain's call the sons of the Empire were rallying round the flag, fighting and dying alongside their British brothers on many battlefields in the defence of freedom. Heroes all. His stirring words brought a thrill of pride to one boy whose father had recently come home on leave wearing on his left breast the ribbon of the Military Medal and on his left arm a golden stripe which denoted that he had been wounded in action.

On the other side of the fence the Mayor's words reminded one girl of a day which recently had changed her whole life. It had started when she was helping to prepare her brother and sisters for school. The postman had delivered a letter from her father who, at the outbreak of war, had marched away with his Territorial Battalion to join Britain's 'Contemptible Little Army', leaving behind his wife and four children. Her mother placed the letter on the mantelpiece to be read when she was alone. After the children had gone to school she decided to do the essential jobs before reading her letter. These being completed she sat at the table and read her husband's letter. He was safe and well. He wrote that he had received a parcel of goodies and cigarettes from Dowlings and Sherwoods and asked her to thank those responsible. He ended by saying he was due for leave very soon. After she had read the letter again she sat a while reminiscing on her happy married life and glowing at the prospect of seeing her husband again.

A knock at the door disturbed her reverie. Wondering, she opened the door. On the doorstep stood a telegraph boy. A prayer came from her heart "O God, no". She took the telegram from his hand, not hearing his condolence "Sorry Missus". She closed the door and returned to the table. Opening the telegram she read the fateful words 'Private A. Smith. Killed in Action'. As she placed her arms on the table the telegram fell to the floor. She thought for a moment and then as she saw her husband's last letter realisation came. The years of hope and dread were over. Now began another era. She and her children were alone. She placed her head in her hands and wept.

Meanwhile the Mayor had concluded his speech. Mr Daniels announced that the County Council had decided not to award the usual medals and shield for regular attendance but the teachers had provided rosettes to mark the occasion. He invited the Mayor to make the presentations and called the following to come forward:

For four years perfect attendance: Frederick Perry, Percy King, Reginald Mitchener.

For three years perfect attendance: Frederick Joyce.

For two years perfect attendance: William Holloway, Albert Blackmore.

For one year perfect attendance: Bertie Bailey, William Fisher, Alfonso Portsmouth.

Four hundred attendances out of a possible 411: Fred Fisher, Stanley Steptoe, Fred Thorne, Hedley Fry, W. Brewer, Edward Synan, Ted Fay, John Selwood, Charles Paice, Frederick Webb, Charles Line, Henry Muggleton, Harry Paris, Albert Holloway, Frederick Parsons.

The Mayoress was then invited to make similar presentations to the girls. Mrs Wells called the following to come forward:

For three years perfect attendance: Evelyn Mitchener.

For two years perfect attendance: Ivy Bevan, Pearl Portsmouth.

Four hundred attendances out of 411: Rose Smith, Rose Aubrey, Ellen Wild, Violet Smith, Ivy Wise, Fanny Hayter, Mildred Paris, Annie Elliot, Muriel

Kendall, Effie Goodyear, Beryl Fry, Maud Aubrey, Annie Wilson, Nellie Dykes, Doris Paris, Kate Dykes, Frances Synan, Gwendoline Mason, Kate Selwood.

The children gave cheers for those who received the awards. The vicar gave a vote of thanks to the Mayor and Mayoress for attending the function and presenting the awards; this was seconded by Rev. Lucas. Mr Daniels spoke on behalf of the children, saying that after the war was over a lot of rebuilding would have to be done in all walks of life and it would call for intelligent men and women. He advised the children to prepare themselves for the future. The Mayor spoke to the children and announced that the rest of the day would be a holiday. Loud cheers from the children.

*

1 April 1918.

The Royal Air Force having been formed, they took over Andover Aerodrome, their blue uniforms creating a splash of colour in a very drab scene. When the RFC became the RAF a women's detachment was formed. A number of Andover women joined. The lived at home and were picked up and conveyed to the aerodrome.

Andover Advertiser. 26 April 1918: Selling cakes to German prisoners. 'By the instructions of the Southern Command the police have summonsed Reginald Bright, a hawker of Amesbury, for selling cakes to German prisoners. The men were working under escort near Boscombe and a witness saw the defendant handing scones to them from a basket. An officer told the county magistrates at Salisbury, who were hearing the case, that it did not seem to be realised that it was a serious crime to sell foodstuffs to prisoners of war. The chairman, Mr L. M. Swayne, said "There is the other side, that the German prisoners are paid too much money and have too much to spend". The defendant was fined £3 which the magistrates hoped his employers would pay.'

In July 1918 agricultural wages were fixed as follows: Carter, Dairyman, Cowman and Shepherd: 37 shillings a week; the hours to be as customary in the Hampshire area. Other male workers: 31 shillings for a 54 hour week in the summer and a 48 hour week in the winter. Overtime rates, 8½ d per hour; Sunday 10d per hour.

*

11 November 1918 was a grey day. The children went to New Street School with a usual Monday morning feeling, but after singing the morning hymn 'Now thank we all our God' a strange sense of anticipation seemed to be in the air. At 11 o'clock the bells of St. Mary's began to ring. All school work was stopped by the three teachers and Mr Noble opened the door dividing the two boys' classrooms and announced that the headmaster would be talking to them. The boys sat silent and upright with their hands folded behind their backs, some of them thinking of their past misdeeds.

Mr Daniels then addressed the whole of the boys' school. He told the boys that the Germans had asked for an armistice which had been signed at 11 o'clock that morning. The whole of the German Army had surrendered and the ceasefire had sounded from the sea to Switzerland. Consequently the immediate fighting was over. After living for over four years in the shadow of war, the boys were slow to respond until Mr Daniels announced that the rest of the day would be a holiday. After a hymn and prayer they gave vent to their feelings as they raced down the street spreading the news.

The boys who passed through the High Street stopped to hear the Mayor make the announcement from the Town Hall window. This was the signal for rejoicing. The flags were hoisted on St. Mary's and the Town Hall, quickly followed by flags and bunting all over the town.

The Mayor, Mr F. Webb, had invited everyone to join him in a celebration procession at 6.0 pm. A small number of bandsmen left in the town, together with the drums and bugles of the Boy Scouts, provided the music and led the procession, followed by the Mayor wearing his chain of office, accompanied by Councillor Bingham and other prominent citizens together with the Local Defence Volunteers and the Fire Brigade. Bringing up the rear was a pair of trucks drawn by a group of Andoverians; on it was mounted an effigy of the Kaiser bearing a placard with the following inscription:

Kaiser Bill you have had your fill
Tis you we all hate
So you must wait
Till half past eight.

The parade circled the centre of the town where the shaded street lighting provided by only half the number of street lamps that had been in operation in 1913, together with torches, storm lanterns, bicycle lamps and carriage lamps provided a flickering illumination. This was augmented at the conclusion of the parade by the flames of the burning effigy in the cobbled market square, to a background of noises from the fireworks and cheering and singing of the people. The banging of petrol tins and anything else that made a noise continued until late in the evening. Those who had the money and the inclination patronised the public houses where the celebrations overflowed into the street.

While all this was going on the Mayor, accompanied by 300 people from various parts of the town, made his way through the revellers to St. Mary's where the Rev. W. Smith conducted a service of thanksgiving and remembrance. The service was bittersweet; joyful with anticipation for those whose loved ones were safe, but sorrowful for those who had received one of those terrible telegrams with the three fatal words 'Killed in Action'. That night their sorrow was shared by all who knew them in the silence that reigned when the names of the fallen were read at the conclusion of the service.

The days that passed after the armistice were eventful. The one question that dominated the scene was 'What now?'.

The prisoners of war were beginning to return, not always to a happy reunion. While the politicians debated the terms to be presented to Germany, men were being demobilised and returning home looking for their old jobs, jobs some had left as boys of 18 encouraged by their employers. They were now returning not only as men, but as men who had proved their worth as leaders of men. They quickly found that this did not entitle them to a job, indeed in some cases even their old job. The same could be said regarding wages. Some employers wished to see a return to the pre-war rates. Once the uniform had been laid aside and 'civvies' were the order of the day it was not what you had been but what you were now that counted.

One family in New Street were overjoyed when they heard that their son was in England. 'Buffer' Rolfe, his wife and family had not received any news of their son Joseph since he was taken prisoner after the five month siege of Kut al Mara in Mesopotamia on 29 April 1916. Since that date, when starving and ill with malaria, dysentery and berri berri, the prisoners had been forced by the Turks to march until they dropped. They were subjected to awful treatment over the years until they were released. His Majesty the King sent the survivors a personal letter of welcome when they returned to England; it reads as follows:

> Buckingham Palace, 1918
>
> No. 32782. Gnr. Rolfe, RFA
> The Queen joins me in welcoming you on your release from the miseries and hardships which you have endured with so much patience and courage. During these many months of trial, the early rescue of our gallant Officers and Men from the cruelties of their captivity has been uppermost in our minds.
> We are thankful that this longed for day has arrived and that back in the old country you will be able once more to enjoy the happiness of home and to see good days among those who anxiously look forward to your return.
>
> George RI

*

14 February 1919. British Red Cross Andover Hospital Supply Depot. 'The Swab and Bandage Depot having been closed down, Mrs Richard and Mrs Berkley wish to thank all those who have worked so well for the Depot, both the regular workers and those who have so often helped to collect funds when necessary, and in many other ways.

Special thanks are due to Mr Percival Clarke who has so kindly lent his premises since May 1916, Miss Dugey for the loan of her furniture, and many others.
Thanks are due to those who have worked so well during 1916-18 and for unavoidable reasons have been unable to continue until the end and thereby earn their badges for Voluntary Service.
A special badge and certificate has been awarded by the Royal Red Cross to Mr P. Clarke.
Since the outbreak of war to the end of 1918, 4526 garments etc were sent to the Red Cross Depot in London for distribution among the Red Cross Hospitals.'

*

Andover Advertiser: 24 October 1919.

'A writer in the *Daily News* had the following things to say in connection with the men of the Hampshire Regiment which will bear repeating:
A short while ago a distinguished general was discussing those questions which civilian acquaintances inevitably inflict upon the 'brass hats'. He had given his opinion of a number of regiments he had seen in action, when he was asked what did he think of the Hampshires. "Well, they won't make Guardsmen" he replied "but for men who will march, march, march and still march, give me the Hampshires". In that phrase you have the essence of the glory of the Hampshires. The marching Hampshires. The solid, good humoured, imperturbable columns which swing down the green lanes of their native county to tramp through half the world. Hampshire is a county of refined and ancient beauty and of ancient survivals. An inviolate storehouse of age long traditions.'

Harry Paris with Southampton's 15th century sword.

In the Southampton Council Chamber there is kept a huge two handed sword forged in the 15th century, which in time of war is always unsheathed. It was drawn on August 4th 1914 and was not put back in the scabbard until the celebration of peace. This ancient sword, naked through all the terrible years, is symbolic of Hampshire. It typifies at once the grim, inflexible determination of those marching battalions and that historic sense which, however veiled, was always with them. As an instance of this subconscious fidelity to the past, let me relate an incident that was told me by a county man who was present at the third battle of Ypres.

The 3rd Battalion was waiting in reserve expecting at any moment to be rushed into the line, but amidst all the fury of that great fight a Hampshire man remembered that it was August 1st, Minden Day. The nearest town was Poperinghe. Thither a messenger sped in quest of red roses, for Minden was won in a rose garden and Hampshire troops celebrate it every year by sporting a red rose in their caps. The envoys found their flowers – they were things of twisted paper but they delighted those staunch Hampshire hearts and in the heat of that day the red roses of the county shone as bravely as at Minden itself.

It is seldom in the history of any regiment that one comes across imaginative touches like this. But such glimpses of historical background help one to understand the peculiar contribution which Hampshire brought into the nation's military effort. There is nothing that is spasmodic about this county. It is concerned with the things that endure. It is difficult to disentangle the Hampshire's record from the great battle story because in tracing one particular battalion the thread is constantly lost in one theatre of war to reappear in another.

Hampshire men had discovered many new horizons in the war years. Of the 7000 and more of the regiment who laid down their lives, there were hundreds of boys who had never previously crossed the borders of their own quiet county but now slept on the beach of Gallipoli, in India, in Mesopotamia and in Siberia.

The 9th Battalion, one of the Territorial units of the Regiment, after spending three years in India were dispatched to Siberia, exchanging a temperature of 115°F for one of 100 degrees below freezing. "See the world is right" observed the bronzed little man who had just been demobilised, referring to the War Office poster "that's what our crowd has been doing for the last five years". He had been wandering through the land of the Arabian Nights since 1915. He was childishly pleased as he emptied his pockets of eastern souvenirs which he had brought home and distributed among his fellow passengers in the railway carriage: an Egyptian cigarette holder cunningly carved out of a fish bone, an Arabic talisman, a coin from the Holy Land.

Although Germany had been granted an armistice and an army of occupation was in that country, the fighting was not over for the Hampshire Regiment as they became involved in the Russian Revolution in Siberia. The news that the vicar's son was reported missing believed killed there was a shock to the town. All extended their sympathies to the vicar and his wife who, although not very robust, was respected for the work she did among the unfortunates of Andover.

Thus it happens that the story of the Hampshire's contribution to the war is one of many chapters. It was a scene constantly changing. Roughly, the main outlines are these:

> Initial honours were won by the 1st Battalion in northern France in 1914.
> The 2nd Battalion, which was out in India at the outbreak of hostilities, won immortal fame amid the mournful splendour of Gallipoli and later played an heroic part in the terrific battles in France from 1916 onwards.
> Of the other Hampshires who were at Gallipoli and the Dardanelles, the 8th (T) went to Egypt and Palestine and the 10th were heard of later in Salonica.
> Most of the Territorial Battalions saw service in the East.
> The single Territorial Battalion (apart from the term troops of other branches of the Service) which saw service in France, was the 2-4th.

Therefore any appreciation of the Hampshires' war service must be divided into three parts: the story of France, the story of Gallipoli and the story of the Eastern Campaign. The same county qualities were tested and revealed in each theatre of war.

*

After the peace, government posts went in the main to ex-servicemen, hundreds of them finding work in the Tidworth area. On the farms and building sites men could be seen wearing parts of their uniforms. One garment they could have returned was their army greatcoat for which every railway station master was authorised to pay each former serviceman £1. Quite a few retained them, as they were entitled to do, and had them dyed.

During the fighting, thousands of soldiers were posted as missing. With the return of the prisoners of war, advertisements were often seen in the press appealing for any information regarding these missing men, but very few received any reply.

Early in February 1919 Enham Village Centre was inaugurated. Four months later 160 disabled ex-servicemen were receiving training there. Travellers passing through the village could not fail to experience a feeling of sympathy for these men who did not regard themselves as heroes but as victims of the curse of war. Some were confined to wheelchairs, others on crutches, some minus an arm or eye, others with no apparent injury but liable at any time to collapse in a screaming fit or worse as a result of shell shock. They moved about the village determined to form themselves into a community and to become independent.

At the end of May 1919 Rothsay Hospital was closed. One thousand three hundred soldiers were patients during the four and a half years it was in operation, among them many colonial soldiers. Mrs Faith, chief organiser, received letters of thanks from the HQ Southern Command and from the War Office to the people of Andover and District who financed it and the ladies who served in the hospital, forty five of whom qualified for a nursing diploma.

*

A committee was formed to organise a Peace Celebration on 18 July 1919. Mr Slinn of the East Street School was the hon. secretary and together with Mr Daniels and Mr Noble of the New Street School he organised the involvement of the schoolchildren. Extra singing lessons were introduced and the streets rang with tunes of national songs as the children sang while playing in the streets.

On the Friday previous to the Saturday fixed for the celebrations, 1500 schoolchildren marched from their schools to St. Mary's Church for a 'Service of Joy', although the scholars from Charlton School were conveyed by farm carts. The service started as a choir of boys led a procession of clergy down the aisle; the vicar was followed by the Rural Dean, Rev. E. R. Allan of Weyhill; Captain Marshall of the Salvation Army; Rev. Lucas, Congregational and Rev. R. Carter, Baptist. The church rang as the children sang their hymns of thanksgiving. In his address the vicar reminded them of the debt they owed to the men and women who had stood between them and the German armies. They were exhorted to be worthy of the sacrifices made on their behalf.

On Saturday morning, 18 July 1919, a procession was formed in The Avenue led by the parade marshal, Mr Sidney Bell, on horseback and flanked by Supt. Cox and Sgt. Collis of the police, followed by the Colours of the old Volunteers which were born by two men dressed in the old Volunteers uniforms. The band of the 14th Hussars headed the local branch of the Comrades of the Great War, bearing their new banner given to them by Mrs Moore and Miss Lynn, and led by Capt. Pollard VC. MC. DCM. Most of them were wearing their Great War medals which, with true army sangfroid, they had nicknamed Pip, Squeak and Wilfred after the characters in the *Daily Mirror* children's cartoons. The Salvation Army band was followed by the representatives of the Friendly Societies with their banners and wearing their sashes of office, and other organisations. The Municipal band provided the music for a long line of decorated vehicles and floats, as well as pedestrians in fancy dress.

The procession passed through crowds of spectators who greeted the Comrades' contingent as they proudly marched to the martial music provided by the Hussars' band. Along Junction Road, Bridge Street, London Street and up East Street they went until the parade marshal turned the corner into Newbury Street. He then found himself faced with a dilemma. This situation had its roots in the years before the war. During

The New Street Peace Fete committee, 1919.
l to r. back row: H. Bunce, A Hinton, G. Turner
middle: G. Portsmouth, Mr Waters, ?, R. Bunce, Mr Connor, A. Tomkins
front: B. Lewis, Miss Durran(?), Miss Bracher, A.S. Dance, H. Burchet, J. Hunter, A. Aubrey.
(HPP34/039)

Mr B. Lewis and family, winners of the best decorated cottage competition, New Street, 1919

The temporary cenotaph in Andover High Street, 1919.
(HPP34/220)

Peace celebration dinner, Andover Drill Hall, 1919.

those years New Street had always been regarded as the slums of Andover and the Newstreeters as the lowest in the social scale, but when the war came the New Street men were foremost in answering the call to the colours and by the end of the war had the highest number of casualties in any one street in the town. Those who returned were different men. No longer were they prepared to accept their lowly status. They had decorated their street as never before and were prepared to join wholeheartedly in the celebrations, but when the processional route was announced they found that once again the prominent citizens of the town had completely ignored New Street.

Some of the street's ex-servicemen approached the organisers requesting that New Street be included in the route. They were told that the arrangements could not be altered. They quietly passed the word around to their comrades and these were the men, wearing their medals, who faced the parade marshal as they had faced their country's enemies for over four years. Lined across Newbury Street, they blocked the way into the High Street. Mr Bell looked around, presumably for police help, but before any action could be taken a man stepped out of the line, backed by a crowd of spectators, and taking the bridle of the parade marshal's horse he led him towards New Street and, with a smack on the animal's rump, dispatched him on his way down the Street amid loud cheers from the Newstreeters. The procession followed. The Newstreeters had made their point. (In later years, when the carnival processions were routed, part of New Street was included.)

Returning from its unexpected visit to the Blacksmiths Arms, the procession made its way to the Town Hall. A wooden monument had been erected just outside the cobbled market place in the centre of the High Street. The lower slopes of the monument were covered with floral tributes to the fallen, ranging from the children's posies to the striking wreath placed by their Comrades. After the marshal had led the saluting march past the monument, the procession dispersed to join the crowds who packed the High Street. The Mayor came to the foot of the monument where he spoke to the crowds and read the Proclamation of Peace. The Comrades and the VAD detachment from Rothsay Hospital then formed ranks and marched away behind the Hussars' band to the Drill Hall, where a feast had been prepared for them. They entered the hall to the applause of those assembled to greet them. Six hundred and fifty sat down to the meal, entertained by music from the Hussars' band.

Afterwards the Mayor addressed them as 'Soldiers of the King' and welcomed them home. He particularly mentioned the VADs who had staffed Rothsay Hospital. The comrades interrupted his speech to give a standing ovation to these ladies, representing as they did the whole military nursing fraternity. This brought blushes to their cheeks and tears to their eyes. He then read this message addressed to them all from the King:

> I desire to express my admiration of the courage and endurance displayed by the Soldiers, Sailors and Airmen of your county during the past five years

New Street peace celebrations, 1919.
(HPP34/105)

Peace celebrations at the Walled Meadow, 1919.
(HPP34/107)

of war. I am grateful to all the brave men and women of the county of Southampton for their devotion and patriotic services. I once more express my sympathy and that of the Queen with the relatives of the gallant men who have given their lives at their country's call and it is our earnest desire and hope that the sick and wounded may be restored to health. I rejoice with you today on the restoration of peace, which I trust will bring to us all unity, contentment and prosperity.

George RI

This message received a tremendous ovation. The Mayor then gave an account of the organisation of the feast and how Mr R. Moore had requested the privilege of providing it. He also welcomed Major Garthwaite from the Enham Village Centre, where great efforts were being made on behalf of their disabled comrades. Major Garthwaite gave a short account of what was being done at the Enham Village Centre. He thanked the organisers for the invitation to the feast received by all the inmates of the Centre. They would certainly have been there but for the fact that the Ministry of Pensions had given them a free ticket to their home town with 10 shillings to enjoy their celebrations, and as was to be expected they had all gone home. After more entertainment, the event closed with the National Anthem.

During the afternoon the crowds began to make their way to the Walled Meadow in the drizzling rain to join the 1600 school children assembled there. The children, conducted by Mr Daniels, sang a programme of patriotic songs accompanied by the Municipal band as follows: Rule Britannia; Australia will be There; The Maple Leaf for Ever; Land of my Fathers; Dear little Shamrock and Auld Lang Syne. During the singing of Australia will be There an Australian soldier, overcome with emotion, climbed on to Mr Daniels' rostrum and joined in the singing. At the end he removed his bush hat and gave three cheers for the children. He then rejoined the crowd who gave him a warm reception. At the conclusion of the singing the children entered the marquees where they were each given a drinking mug decorated with the flags of the Allies. They sat down to a tea, catered for by Mr T. Lock of New Street.

The rain having become very heavy, it was decided to postpone the children's sports until Monday. During the evening the rain cleared and at 10 o'clock torches were issued to adults from the Town Hall and, having lit them from a bonfire in the market square, they joined the procession behind the Municipal band and the Mayor. When all was ready they marched away round the town centre and up Old Winton Road to Bere Hill where, jealously guarded, stood a heap of inflammable material some 20 feet high. Amidst the crack of fireworks the Mayor, with the aid of a torch, fired the bonfire. The flames rose high in the sky, colouring the dark grey clouds. This was the signal for other bonfires on the high points around the town to be lit. Soon Andover was at the centre of a ring of fires.

As the fire died down the band played the National Anthem and the spectators wandered homewards, some children pick-a-back, tired out after their wonderful day and perhaps not realising what an awful period in their country's history had just ended and what a price had still to be paid. But they were happy in the togetherness of the Andoverians on Peace Celebration Day, 18th July 1919.

*

After the peace celebrations, the Andoverians expressed their desire to erect a permanent memorial to the men who gave their lives in the war. A public meeting was called and suggestions asked for; they ranged from a statue in the High Street to stained glass windows in St. Mary's. Eventually it was suggested that a new, modern hospital should be built. Various gentlemen expressed the view that this suggestion, desirable as it was, was too ambitious. It would be too heavy for the ratepayers to carry – and where would it be built? Another view was that a hospital would be on the outskirts of the town when what was desired was a memorial in the centre for all to see. A committee was formed to investigate the possibilities and report back.

When the news spread that a new hospital was contemplated, offers of help and finance came from various organisations throughout the district. Mr Henry Gamman offered as a gift a site of three acres in Charlton Road which would allow for future development. Mr Wells offered to give an acre of land in the Weyhill Road near the Tavern. If it was agreed that the site offered by Mr Wells was the most suitable, Mr Gamman offered to buy and present a hundred feet frontage to the Weyhill Road, bringing the site up to one and three quarter acres. After inspecting the sites, it was recommended that the Charlton Road offer should be accepted.

The committee reported back with this information and an estimation of £15000 to build a hospital. Those who favoured a monument asked if it was possible to have both. Eventually it was decided that both the monument and the hospital would be built, the latter to be known as the Andover and District War Memorial Hospital. A building fund was to be set up and contributors were to mark their donations H or M, whichever was their desire. Those on the monument committee were: Rev. W. Smith, S. Bell, W. P. Clark, B. Lamb, H. C. McLoughlin, R. T. Moore, A. E. Daniels, C. J. Middleton, J. T. Pankhurst and E. J. Slinn, with Captain Cowley, architect.

All the organisations in the district set to work with a will to raise the required money. Events were staged and a jazz band toured the district, being warmly welcomed as they paraded through the village streets. A group of young gentlemen pushed and played a barrel organ for miles as their part of the general effort. School children were invited to buy a brick for twopence. A grand carnival was organised. It was noticeable that 'the' hospital soon became 'our' hospital as everyone rallied round. After invited tenders had been considered, it was decided that the monument should be built by H. W. Page of Andover and the hospital by Musslewhite and Sons of Basingstoke.

On 19 April 1920 the Andover War Memorial stood in the High Street ready for the unveiling ceremony. A platform stood in front of the monument and before it was an enclosure for the school children. The mourners were seated on each side of the monument. Massed choirs led the singing to organ music played by Mr Farmar and Mr Edwards. The High Street was filled with the local populace. The Municipal band, playing the Dead March in Saul, headed the procession from the Town Hall which was led by the vicar and all the religious leaders of the town. The Mayor, Alderman F. Webb, and the Corporation then took their places on the platform. On the steps of the memorial stood eight trumpeters of the Irish Dragoon Guards.

Ald. H. C. McLoughlin welcomed the Lord Lieutenant of Hampshire, who inspected the Guard of Honour provided by the 4th Irish Dragoon Guards. The vicar conducted a short service which concluded with the reading of the Roll of the Dead, numbering 213 men. Major General J. E. B. Seeley then addressed the gathering, his theme being thankfulness that the war was over and the hope that as we had striven together and these men had died to win the war, we should still band together to win the peace and make our community worthy of the sacrifice made by our townsmen.

Leaving the platform amid a silence broken only by the sobbing of some of the mourners, he ascended the steps surrounding the cenotaph and unveiled the memorial. The vicar joined him and in the name of the Deity blessed the memorial. The trumpeters then sounded the Last Post. Various dignitaries laid wreaths on the memorial and the ceremony closed with the National Anthem. Hundreds of floral tributes were then laid by relatives and friends of those whose names were to be found on the cenotaph.

One item on the monument raised considerable interest. This stated that the conflict lasted from 1914 to 1920, although the official date for the ending of the war was 11 November 1918. The reason for this was that Andover men served in Russia until January 1920 during the time of the revolution. They had been serving in India with the 9th Battalion of the Hampshire Regiment, which was a Territorial unit equipped with bicycles; they wore a blue wheel depicting a cycle in the lapel of their tunics. When the Russian revolution broke out in 1917, the Hampshires were sent to serve with the Russian army which was still engaged in fighting the Germans. The battalion left Siberia in January 1920 to return to this country where they were disbanded and demobilised. The Treaty of Peace was ratified on 10 January 1920 by Order in Council.

*

On 15 June 1925 a long line of cars was to be seen in the High Street. At a given time it moved towards the Town Hall where a group of local dignitaries and their wives were waiting. They were driven to the building site in Charlton Road where the foundations of the Andover War Memorial Hospital were being prepared. There they seated themselves with others on a platform sheltered by a brightly coloured awning. Among them were Col. A. Holbrook, Mr and Mrs E. Parsons, Mr and Mrs H. Gamman,

Dedication of the War Memorial, 1920.

Andover War Memorial.

Sir A. and Lady Yarrow, Mrs D. Farr, Mr and Mrs Pankhurst, Miss Puty, Miss E. M. Bracher, Mr E. Maufe and Mr L. Moore, joint architects. Grouped at the sides of the platform were children from all the local Sunday Schools and their teachers. Clergy from the Andover Deanery and nonconformist leaders and pastors were grouped together. A united choir drawn from local choirs led the singing to music provided by the Municipal band. A detachment of the VAD was present.

Dr E. A. Farr, chairman of the Hospital Building Committee, left the platform to welcome the Lord Lieutenant of Hampshire, Maj. Gen. Seeley, and the Bishop of Winchester. A guard of honour provided by 50 men and their officers from the Wiltshire Regiment was inspected by the Lord Lieutenant and a short service was led by the Rural Dean. The Lord Lieutenant then laid the foundation stone and addressed the gathering saying how honoured he was, after having unveiled the cenotaph in the High Street, to be asked to lay this foundation stone of such a worthy objective. It would be a fitting memorial to those who gave their all. The Bishop of Winchester blessed the stone, saying how he gloried in the decision to erect this hospital and in the efforts of the community in Andover and District to raise the money to enable the hospital to open free from debt; it was surely an outstanding endeavour. The Mayor of Andover thanked the distinguished guests for their attendance which was appreciated by everyone.

The concluding event of the afternoon was to have been the laying of offerings on the foundation stone by the Sunday School children, but they were diverted by the crush of people who surged forward to inspect the stone. In the event, £300 was deposited on the stone to help swell the fund which aimed to reach £15000. (Once that was accomplished the Building Committee would be able to call on a certain gentleman to make good his offer of £500 and so make it possible to open the hospital free from debt.)

*

The 26 June 1926 was momentous for the Andoverians and the New Streeters in particular as the Prince of Wales was to pass through their street on the way to Enham Village Centre to open the Landale Wilson Institute. The New Streeters were determined to show their loyalty with their decorations and started their preparations on the Monday. Unfortunately their spirits were dampened a little when it was learned that Arthur Aubrey's little daughter had been involved in an accident. She ran across the road behind a string of stone carts and collided with a car being driven in the opposite direction. The driver took her to the new hospital where she was found to be suffering from a broken thigh and other injuries.

Nothing daunted, the task of decorating the street was completed and when the Prince arrived, after his official welcome by the Mayor, Ald. R. Kendal, at a ceremony on the Town Hall forecourt, the New Streeters lined their street and met him with ringing cheers. Not perhaps a great display but one which came from the heart and was all their very own.

Having completed his visit to Enham, the Prince returned to the railway station via Charlton. He broke his journey to inspect the Andover and District War Memorial Hospital and toured the wards, speaking to the patients. He made enquiries about little Miss Aubrey, which was much appreciated by the New Streeters, and offered his congratulations to the people of Andover and District on their wonderful achievement in offering a fine hospital as a memorial to the fallen. His last duty as a visitor was to be the first to sign the Visitors Book, proudly watched by the President of the hospital, Mrs Jenkins, and Dr E. A. Farr. Shortly after this visit Kathy Aubrey received a signed photograph of HRH The Prince of Wales, as did the other patients in residence.

The hospital was officially opened four days later, on June 30th, when large crowds took up their positions to watch the event. The building provided a fitting backdrop on a sunny afternoon, the sunshine picking out the red and white pennants on the lances of the Guard of Honour, the gay bunting surrounding the platform set up in the recess in the front of the hospital and reflecting on the helmets of the Fire Brigade on parade.

The crowd covered the green sward extending to Charlton Road. Amid their cheers Dr Farr welcomed Field Marshal Lord Allenby who proceeded to inspect the Guard of Honour provided by the 16/5 Lancers, who had received this honour twice before during the Field Marshal's service in Egypt. The inspection completed, Lord

Lord Allenby at the opening of the Andover War Memorial Hospital, 1926.

Allenby extended his congratulations to the bandmaster of the 2nd Battalion Welsh Regiment and then, escorted by Dr Farr, proceeded to the platform followed by the Mayor and Corporation. A service was held in which leaders of all the religious bodies took part, with massed choirs leading the hymn singing.

Lord Allenby then addressed the crowd, reminding them of the purpose of their presence and congratulating the people of Andover and District on their choice of memorial and mentioning the relations, friends and comrades of those who had made the supreme sacrifice. Not only that but also the worthy work done by local people who in seven months had schemed and raised the money to enable the hospital to be opened free from debt. He congratulated the architects, Mr Maufe and Mr Moore, and the builders, Musslewhite & Sons of Basingstoke. Mr Maufe then presented the key to Lord Allenby who left the platform and proceeded to the hospital's main doors which he unlocked, declaring the hospital open. He returned to the platform to receive a vote of thanks for his services from Mr Parsons.

Dr Farr fulfilled a life long ambition when he handed over the hospital to the matron, Miss Emery. Sir Arthur Holbrook MP thanked the Building Committee. A procession of visitors then approached the main doors and after handing over purses to the matron they passed through the hospital waving to the eleven patients in residence.

*

Abbreviations used:

ASC	Army Service Corps
BEF	British Expeditionary Force
DLI	Durham Light Infantry
NCO	non-commissioned officer
RFA	Royal Field Artillery
RFC	Royal Flying Corps
TA	Territorial Army

Andover Junction Station was the present Andover Station.

AN INDEX OF SOME WELL KNOWN ANDOVERIANS OF THE NINETEENTH CENTURY

Compiled by Andrew Jackson

Allen	Nathaniel	b 1840. Landlord of Forester's Arms.
Allen	S H	Hospital Committee.
Andrews	Wilfred	1873-1949. Mineral water manufacturer in Marlborough Street - Empire Works. Well known campanologist in Winchester.
Annett	Arthur	1815-1892. Builder.
Annett	Henry	b 1825. Master builder.
Anthony	Edward	b 1836. Cemetery keeper.
Archer	Charles	b 1836. Coal merchant.
Ash	Frederick John	b 1855. Draper. Debating society committee. Director of Andover Penny Bank. Council member 1879-1882.
Atkins	Alfred Edward	Choral society committee.
Audry	Revd. W H	Rector of Ludgershall. Supporter of cottage hospital.
Baker	James	Currier. Soup and coal fund. Council member in 1835.
Banks	Thomas Alexander	b 1823. Innkeeper at the Chequers. Speculative builder. Charged with the murder of William Parsons in 1858. Acquitted.
Banning	Frederick	b 1826. Blacksmith.
Barclay	George Henry	1837-1910. Manager of the London and County Bank. Treasurer and chairman of the Institute 1876-1879. Debating society committee.
Barnes	George	1758-1832. Director of Andover Savings Bank. Corporation member 1805-1832.
Barnes	Henry	Subscriber to the Andover Institute.
Barnes	John	b 1825. Baker.
Barnes	Samuel	1852. Solicitor's clerk.
Barnes	Walter	Plumber. Debating society committee.
Barnes	William	Corporation member 1833-1834.
Beach	W W	MP. Supported the soup and coal fund.
Beale	Frank	b 1843. Builder. Institute committee. Supporter of the cottage hospital.
Beale	Francis Arthur	b 1877. Son of Frank. Builder. Captain of the fire brigade 1892-1935.
Beare	William G	b 1842. Music seller.
Beck	John	b 1837. Debating society committee
Bennett	William	b 1822. Music teacher. First conductor of the choral society in 1860.

Bensley	John Benjamin	Printer in Soper's lane c. 1825.
Bentall	Francis	Subscriber to the Institute. Jury member to enquire into the death of William Parsons who had been murdered 1858.
Best	Hon. Revd. Samuel	1802-1873. Rector of Abbots Ann 1831-1873. Educationalist. Institute committee member. Chairman of the Andover Savings Bank.
Betteridge	George	b 1845. Innkeeper of the Southampton Arms.
Bienvenu	John	d 1905. Debating society committee.
Bignell	Samuel	b 1817. Accountant. Director of Andover Savings Bank.
Bishop	Robert Owen	Headmaster at the grammar school 1905-1925.
Blake	Charles	b 1847. Manager of the Catherine Wheel coffee house.
Bloxham	Fitzherbert	b 1861. Director of the gas company in 1905. Captain of the fire brigade 1894-1899.
Blunt	Edward Walter	Trustee of the Andover Savings Bank.
Blunt	James	Director of the Andover Savings Bank.
Bosanquet	Henry	Director of the Andover Savings Bank.
Bousfield	Henry Brougham	Vicar of Andover 1870-1878. Institute committee. Suggested the pest house be converted into a hospital. Cottage hospital committee member. Soup and coal fund.
Bracher	Henry James	JP. Councillor. First librarian of the Institute. Soup and coal fund.
Bracher	William	b 1832. Eastanton farm. Mayor 1890. Director of Catherine Wheel Coffee House Ltd. Cottage hospital committee. Soup and coal fund. Councillor 1892-1895.
Brackstone	Joseph	b 1834. Licensee of the Plough Inn.
Braithwaite	Philip Richard	Vicar of Andover 1899-1901. On the jury to enquire into the death of William Parsons who was murdered in 1858.
Bramley	Abraham	d 1853. Watchmaker.
Bramley	Thomas	1824-1903. Watch and clock maker. Made the clock for the toll house on Western Hill which was later moved to the Institute.

Brewer	John George	Saddler. Original shareholder in the gas company. On the jury to enquire into the death of William Parsons who was murdered in 1858.
Brewer	W H	Secretary of Andover Savings Bank.
Bridger	William Fowler	Director of gas company in 1838 . Councillor in 1835.
Briggs	Col. J P	Subscriber to the soup and coal fund.
Broad	George	d 1838. Licensee of the Catherine Wheel in 1830. Councillor in 1835. Lighting and pavement commissioner.
Broad	Jane	Wife of George. Licensee in 1839.
Brooks	Richard	b 1831. Lower Wyke Down farm.
Brown	Henry	Gas works engineer in 1847.
Brown	J	Gas works manager in 1852.
Brown	John Burgiss	Bought the Andover Advertiser from J R Fox in 1868.
Browne	Charles	Manager of the gas company 1840-1871. Institute committee.
Browne	Frederick John James	1827-1896. Bookseller. Institute librarian 1877. Secretary of choral society. Supporter of the cottage hospital. Started the Andover Times in 1858. It ceased in 1912. On the jury which enquired into the death of William Parsons who was murdered in 1858.
Buckland	Lander	b 1844. Draper.
Bull	Luke	b 1819. Master chimney sweep.
Bull	Thomas	Council member 1878-1881.
Bulpitt	George	b 1825. Licensee of the Red Lion.
Bunce	John	b 1826. Tea dealer.
Bunce	Henry	b 1841. Licensee of the Bell and Crown, Hatherden.
Burley	George	b 1829. Draper.
Butt	Thomas	Subscriber to the Institute.
Butterworth	Alfred	1833-1913. Owned Hatherden estate and a cotton mill in Oldham. In 1897 he gave £500 towards the purchase of the Institute for use as a free library. Shareholder in the Catherine Wheel Coffee House Ltd.
Buxton	Francis William	1847-1910. Liberal MP for Andover 1880-1885

Caldecott	John Devon	d 1905. Shareholder in the Catherine Wheel Coffee House. For many years he was treasurer of the soup and coal fund.
Callow	Henry	b 1811. Seedsman.
Carey	John	b 1813. Tenant of Charlton farm.
Carey	Thomas	b 1845. Councillor 1891-1894.
Chaddock	Lucy E	b 1846. Matron of cottage hospital.
Chamberlain	Edward	Gunsmith. Councillor 1891-1894.
Cheales	Henry	b 1797. Clergyman.
Chevis	James	b 1829. Perfumier. Shareholder in gas company.
Child	Charles	b 1815. Brewer.
Child	Revd. T	Vicar of Clatford. Supporter of cottage hospital. Councillor 1883-1886.
Church	Jane	b 1856. Wax flower seller.
Chuter	John William	1844-1901. Music teacher. Organist at St Mary's. Conductor of choral society. Mayor 1892. Debating society committee. Councillor 1885-1894. Alderman 1891-1894.
Clark	Arthur	b 1850. Gunsmith. Debating society committee.
Clark	George	b 1836. Draper. Mayor 1891. Guardian of the poor. Institute committee in 1879. Debating society. Director of Andover Penny Bank. Councillor 1883-1895.
Clark	Henry	b 1843. Licensee of the Pheasant Inn.
Clark	John	b 1830. Postmaster at Charlton.
Clark	William	1826-1897. Grocer. Mineral water manufacturer. Subscriber to the Institute. On jury to enquire into the death of William Parsons who was murdered in 1858.
Clarke	Edward	Secretary of the gas company in 1881. Debating society committee. Director of Andover Savings Bank.
Clarke	Turner Poulter	1803-1897. JP. Mayor 1854, 1858, 1863, 1866 and 1875. Surveyor of Andover. Receiver and manager of the Itchen Navigation company. Lighting and pavement commissioner.
Clayton	Charles F	b 1856. Curate of Enham and Smannell.

Cockerill	Thomas	1734-1813. Surveyor of windows. Corporation member 1783-1813.
Cockings	John Woodward	1833-1900. Goldsmith.
Coggin	Arthur W V	b 1857. Prudential Assurance agent.
Colebrook	Samuel	b 1830. Licensee of the British Oak, Smannell.
Cole	Robert (elder)	Headmaster of the grammar school 1812-1835.
Cole	Robert (younger)	Headmaster of the grammar school 1835-1838.
Coles	Henry Beaumont	1794-1862. of Middleton. MP for Andover 1847-1856. Director of Andover Savings Bank.
Coles	Mary Ann	b 1827. Licensee of the Star Hotel.
Collier	Charles	Vicar 1878-1889. Chairman of the Institute. Chairman of the hospital committee. Director of Andover Savings Bank.
Compton	Thomas Henry Edward	1837-1917. Corn and seed merchant. Guardian of the poor in 1894. Director of the Catherine Wheel Coffee House and shareholder. Supporter of the cottage hospital. Shareholder in Andover Waterworks Ltd. Councillor 1891-1894.
Coombs	Thomas W A	b 1839. Corn merchant.
Cooper	Henry	1852-1890. Licensee of the Royal Oak, Charlton. Committed suicide.
Coote	A	Director of the Catherine Wheel Coffee House Ltd.
Cope	Revd. Alfred D	Headmaster of the grammar school 1874-1880.
Cornwall	C W	Conductor of the choral society in 1870.
Cotes	Peter	Director of the Andover Savings Bank.
Cox	Richard Bethel	Trustee of Andover Savings Bank.
Criswick	Charles	Corporation member 1825-1833.
Criswick	George	b 1791. Corporation member 1823-1832.
Criswick	Henry	Grocer. Churchwarden. Valued the Catherine Wheel in 1811. Corporation member 1812-1835. Lighting and pavement commissioner in 1840.
Cross	Reuben	b 1822. Brewer. Conductor of the choral society in 1871.

Cubitt	William	1791-1863. Subscriber to the Institute. Liberal MP for Andover 1847-1863.
Culling	John	b 1859. Landlord of the Rose and Chequer 1896-1919.
Curtis	George	b 1829. Brewer. Council member 1878-1881. Mayor 1880.
Curtis	Sir Lucas	Trustee of Andover Savings Bank.
Daniel	William	b 1858 Policeman.
Davis	Charlotte	b 1848. Licensee of the Blacksmith's Arms.
Davis	Thomas	Director of Andover Savings Bank.
Deane	Edward	b 1842. Licensed victualler in Chantry Street.
Dickman	Henry	b 1841. Beer seller in Charlton.
Dixon	Revd. J	Cottage hospital committee.
Dodman	Forby	Postmaster of Andover 1855-1875.
Dodson	Revd. Christopher	Turnpike trustee. First chairman of Board of Guardians, 1835.
Dowling	Henry	b 1827. JP. Grocer. Mayor 1872. Director of gas company and shareholder. Guardian of the poor. Shareholder in Catherine Wheel Co Ltd. Museum curator. Subscriber to the Institute. Choral society committee. Director of Andover Penny Bank. Soup and coal committee. Opened the swimming pool in 1895. Director of Andover Waterworks. Lighting and pavement commissioner.
Dowling	John	Appointed head constable in 1842 at £1 pw.
Dowling	Robert	1813-1884. Wine merchant. Director and shareholder in gas company. Mayor 1874. Subscriber to the Institute. Choral society committee. Cottage hospital supporter.
Dowling	Thomas	1852-1925. Ironmonger. Director of Andover Penny Bank.
Drew	Robert	Jury member to enquire into the death of William Parsons who was murdered in 1858.
Drover	William P	Shareholder in gas company.

Dudley	Hon. Francis Fortescue	1820-1909. Subscriber to the Institute. Andover MP 1867-1874.
Dugey	George	1832-1904. Councillor.
Dunn	Frederick	Boot and shoemaker. On jury to enquire into the death of William Parsons who was murdered in 1858.
Dynham	Revd. William Henry	Headmaster of the grammar school 1873-1874.
Dyson	Revd. Francis	Director of Andover Savings Bank.
Dyson	John	Subscriber to the Institute. Lighting and pavement commissioner. On jury to enquire into the death of William Parsons who was murdered in 1858.
Earle	Henry	Attorney. Director of Andover Savings Bank. Corporation member 1833-1835. Council member 1835. Mayor in 1839.
Earle	William Henry	b 1814. Mayor 1845, 1856 and 1865. Director of gas company. Owned the Globe in 1863. Subscriber to the Institute. Lighting and pavement commissioner.
Edwards	E M	b 1841. Congregational minister.
Edwards	Henry	1852-1916. Grocer. Mayor 1887 and 1888. Chairman of soup and coal fund. Councillor 1883-1895.
Ellen	Frederick Charles	1855-1900. Estate agent. Alderman 1889-1898. Mayor 1894. Subscriber to the Institute. Chairman of the Water works company.
Elliott	Dr. Frederick Henry	President of the debating society. In 1878 he demonstrated the telephone from his house in London Street to the Guildhall.
Elliott	Dr. Jabez Henry	b 1824 Mayor 1869.
Etwall	Ralph	Corporation member 1783-1832. Town clerk until 1813. Director of Andover Savings Bank,
Etwall	Ralph (junior)	Director of Andover Savings Bank. Andover MP 1831-1847.
Evans	Revd. Robert	Turnpike trustee.
Everett	James Hague	Director of Andover Savings Bank.
Eyles	G C	Builder. Supporter of the cottage hospital.

Farr	Dr. Septimus Briggs	1839-1898. Shareholder in Catherine Wheel Coffee House. First medical officer for Andover.
Farr	Dr. Ernest Augustus	Hospital committee. Medical officer for Andover. Said to have owned the first car in Andover.
Fellowes	Hon. Newton	Andover MP 1802-1820. Corporation member 1793-1835.
Fennell	Samuel	1722-1802. Silversmith and auctioneer. Corporation member 1753-1801.
Fennell	William B	1754-1831. Corporation member 1776-1828.
Fenwick	Revd. J B	Vicar of Abbots Ann. Hospital committee.
Fermor	Charles Anthony	Largest shareholder in gas company.
Festing	Henry I	Corporation member 1804-1808.
Festing	Henry II	Corporation member 1814-1828.
Flander/Fiander	William	Landlord of the Boro Arms.
Footner	Harry L	1808-1884. Solicitor. Secretary, director and shareholder of the gas company. Choral society committee. Soup and coal fund. Last deputy steward and town clerk of the old corporation. First town clerk of the new borough in 1835.
Footner	Richard	b 1777. Deputy steward and town clerk 1813-1833.
Footner	Richard	1837-1894. Solicitor. Subscriber to the Institute and committee member. Supporter of the cottage hospital. Lighting and pavement commissioner. Town Clerk 1875-1885.
Footner	S C	Mayor 1899.
Forster	Paul	b 1843. Barrister.
Fowle	William H	Subscriber to the Institute. Bankrupt in 1885. His wife owned Pitts Mill and complained about sewage in the Anton.
Fox	Frederick	b 1814. Fishmonger.
Fox	John Russell	Started the Andover Advertiser in 1857. Soup and coal fund. On jury to enquire into the murder of William Parsons in 1858.
Fox	Robert	Subscriber to the Institute.
Fox	William	b 1821. Watchmaker.

Fraser	H P	Debating society committee.
French	George	b 1822. In charge of the pest house.
Frost	George	Subscriber to the Institute.
Frowd	Revd. Edward	Subscriber to the Institute. Chairman of the Andover Savings Bank.
Fryer	Revd. G A	Debating society committee. Soup and coal fund
Futcher	Francis Stephen	b 1853. Draper. Shareholder in the Catherine Wheel Coffee House Ltd.
Gale	John	b 1841. Farmer in Smannell. Councillor
Gale	Martha	1773-1863. Andover benefactor. Niece of Dr W S Goddard who rebuilt St Mary's.
Gamerk	Walter	b 1850. Landlord of Angel Inn.
Gamester	Robert	b 1815. Beadle.
Gamman	Henry	Owner of Pitts Mill which he renamed Anton Mill. d 1926
Garrett	Pink	Councillor in 1835. Lighting and pavement commissioner.
Gawler	Henry	Ramridge House. Director of Andover Savings Bank.
Gibbons	G	Installed a telephone line from Weyhill brewery to his office in Bridge Street.
Gibbs	William	Stone mason. Contractor when the Guildhall was rebuilt in 1825.
Gilbert	Albert Thomas	b 1848. Solicitor's clerk.
Gilbert	Thomas	Corporation member 1796-1809.
Gilbert	William	Council member 1835.
Goddard	William Stanley	1757-1845. Headmaster of Winchester College. Trustee of Andover Savings Bank. Demolished Andover's Saxon church and rebuilt it.
Godden	John II	1730-1814. Corporation member 1760-1808.
Godden	John III	1761-1839. Corporation member 1794-1834.
Godden	John IV	Corporation member 1833-1835.
Gooden	George J R	b 1832. Landlord of Railway Hotel.
Gooden	John	Surveyor in 1838.
Goodluck	John	b 1819. Licensee of Elephant Inn.
Goodinge	John Mills	Subscriber to Institute. Lighting and pavement commissioner.
Goss	W	Debating society committee.

Gould	Robert George	b 1851. Chemist. Debating society committee.
Gradidge	William	b 1855. Chemist, photographer, mineral water manufacturer. Treasurer of debating society.
Greene	Revd. H B	Trustee of Andover Savings Bank.
Greenly	Revd. John	Headmaster of grammar school 1810-1812.
Gregory	Jane E	b 1836. Principal of Weyhill Road boarding school.
Gue	William	1800-1877. Builder. Mayor 1870 and 1871. Subscriber to Institute. Gave site for the cottage hospital. Lighting and pavement commissioner. Town surveyor in 1838. On jury to enquire into the death of William Parsons. Portrait in Guildhall.
Guyatt	George	b 1798. Blacksmith.
Hadden	John	b 1821. Rooksbury mill.
Hall	Walter	Mineral water manufacturer in Bridge Street.
Hammans	Henry	1831-1901. Alderman 1880-1898. Mayor 1877, 1881 and 1883. On hospital committee.
Hammans	C	Mayor 1905.
Hampton	Lewis	b 1840. Millwright.
Harley	Thomas	Director of gas company.
Harrison	Revd. John	Headmaster of grammar school 1844-1873. Director of Andover Savings Bank. Soup and coal fund.
Hart	Thomas	b 1850. Draper, Parsons & Hart.
Hasler	Revd. Joseph	b 1830. Baptist minister. Guardian of the poor. Supporter of cottage hospital. Soup and coal fund. Colporteur committee.
Hawker	Peter	Director of Andover Savings Bank.
Hawkins	Benjamin	b 1825. Timber merchant. Mayor 1859.
Hawkins	Edward Bishop	b 1810. Millwright. Subscriber to Institute. Lighting and pavement commissioner.
Hawkins	Edward Thomas	Subscriber to Institute.
Hawkins.	Revd. H	Cottage hospital committee.

Hayes	Edward	Subscriber to Institute. Lighting and pavement commissioner.
Hayes	George	Council member 1878-1881.
Hayton	William	b 1835. Brewer.
Healey	Richard	1727-1808. Tanner. Corporation member 1786-1807.
Heath	Alan Borman	Sold Catherine Wheel for £900 for use as the Institute. Subscriber to the Institute. Treasurer of Andover Savings Bank.
Heath	Charles	Dealer and banker.
Heath	Thomas	Mayor 1837. Shareholder and director of gas company.
Heath	William Hawkins	Banker. Mayor 1840. Owner of the Catherine Wheel. Treasurer of Andover Savings Bank. Corporation member 1817-1835. Council member 1835-1844.
Heathcote	Gilbert	Vicar of Andover 1811-1829.
Helsdon	C V	Choral society committee.
Hendy	Edward Francis	1832-1899. Hospital committee.
Herbert	Alfred	Painter and glazier. Subscriber to Institute. On jury to enquire into the death of William Parsons who was murdered in 1858.
Herbert	Charles	1831-1894. Coach builder. Alderman 1880-1886. Mayor 1876 and 1885. Subscriber to Institute. Soup and coal fund. Guardian of the poor.
Hewitt	Joseph Grace	b 1823. Harness maker. Debating society committee. On jury to enquire into the death of William Parsons who was murdered in 1858.
Hewitt	William	Shareholder in Catherine Wheel Coffee Company. Shareholder in gas company.
Hilary	John	Subscriber to Institute.
Hobbs	Benjamin	Shareholder in Andover Waterworks.
Holloway	John	Tenant of Pitts Mill. Mayor 1847. Lighting and pavement commissioner. Council member 1835.

Holmes	James Charles	1826-1908. Stationer. Bought Andover Advertiser from J B Brown in 1876. Shareholder and director of gas Company. Institute committee. Debating society committee. Director of Andover Penny Bank.
Hooper	Albert Frederick	b 1845. Auctioneer's clerk. Institute committee. Shareholder in gas company.
Howard	Thomas	Choral society committee.
Howley	William	Vicar of Andover 1801-1811.
Humpherey	William Henry	1827-1909. Andover MP 1863-1867.
Hunt	Robert	b 1837. Inland revenue officer. Councillor.
Hurford	William	Tailor. Cottage hospital committee.
Iremonger	William H	JP. of Wherwell Priory. Cottage hospital committee. Turnpike trustee.
Jackson	William	b 1821. Wesleyan minister.
James	Frederick John	Bookseller. Secretary of Andover Waterworks Ltd.
Jarvis	James	b 1833. Licensee of Globe hotel.
Jerome	Charles	b 1829. Coach builder.
Jonas	G W	Subscriber to the Institute. First treasurer of cottage hospital.
Judd	John	b 1851. Finkley farm.
Kebbell	Revd. C D	Subscriber to the Institute. Director of Andover Savings Bank. Soup and coal fund.
Keeping	G J	Postmaster 1913-1919.
Kellow	Charles William	b 1833. Corn merchant. Director of gas company. Shareholder and chairman of Catherine Wheel Coffee House Ltd. Director of Andover Waterworks Ltd.
Kellow	John	Surveyor in 1838
Killick	Miss H	First matron of cottage hospital.
Kimber	George	b 1844. Police sergeant.
Kimble		b 1841. Licensee of Spotted Dog.
King	Charles	Shareholder in gas company.
Kirby	John	b 1842. Hawker. Lived in a travelling van in a meadow.

Knapp	Robert Walter	Council surveyor 1901-1920.
Lamb	Thomas	1843-1906. Solicitor. Shareholder in gas company. Subscriber to the Institute.
Lambden	Charles	b 1836. Licensee of the King's Head.
Lambden	John Robert	Leased part of the Catherine Wheel.
Lambert	Revd. A	Trustee of Andover Savings Bank.
Lambert	Emile A'Speculo	b 1845. French teacher.
Lane	Revd. H T	Soup and coal fund.
Langstaff	Thomas	1785-1852. Druggist. Organist at St. Mary's. Member of Corporation 1828-1835.
Langstaff	William	Original councillor in 1835. Lighting and pavement commissioner.
Lansley	William	Carpenter. Worked on the rebuilding of the Guildhall in 1825.
Latham	Robert T	1808-1896. Surgeon and apothecary. Mayor 1868.
Lavington	Thomas Richard	b 1835. Manager of Capital & Counties Bank. Auditor of Catherine Wheel Coffee House Ltd. Cottage hospital committee.
Leach	George	b 1835. First colporteur in Andover.
Lee	John	b 1841. Tailor. Mayor 1888. On Institute committee. Choral society committee. Debating society committee.
Leedham	William	Subscriber to the Institute.
Leversuch	Ruchard II	1745-1806. Corporation member 1771-1804.
Levy	Revd. Thomas	Subscriber to the Institute. Debating society committee.
Longman	Thomas Edgar	b 1853. Solicitor. Treasurer of the Institute. Debating society committee. Town Clerk 1885-1930. Councillor 1885-1894.
Longstaff	Thomas	Corporation member 1828-1835.
Longstaff	William	Chemist. Council member 1835.
Loscombe	Francis Russell	1816-1887. Supporter of the cottage hospital.

Loscombe	Henry Albert	Solicitor. Trustee of the Institute and subscriber. Soup and coal fund. Lighting and pavement commissioner. Prosecuted Thomas Banks for the murder of William Parsons in 1858. Banks was found not guilty.
Loscombe	Wintringham	JP. Member of the corporation 1817-1835.
Ludlow	William	Grocer and wine and spirit merchant. Member of the corporation 1805-1835.
Lynn	Thomas	b 1844. Ironmonger.
Lywood	E	Choral society committee.
Macklin	Henry Thomas Percy	b 1855. Tobacconist.
Madgwick	William B	1839-1891. Chemist. Director of gas company. Institute committee.
Madgwick	Rufus	1845-1904. Brother of William. Shareholder in gas company.
Mair	John	b 1810. Curator of museum. Director of Andover Penny Bank.
Major	William	Mayor 1842 and 1850. Director and shareholder in gas company. Corporation member 1834-1835. Council member 1835.
Mann	Thomas	Attorney. Council member 1835.
Marcer	Richard	Corporation member 1807-1808. Postmaster 1780-1803 and possibly again in 1809.
Marcer	George William	Postmaster in 1832.
Marchment	Henry	b 1822. Farmer in Charlton.
Marchment	Charles	b 1856. Farmer in Charlton.
Marsh	Annie	b 1822. Innkeeper.
Marsh	Matthew Henry	Subscriber to the Institute. Turnpike trustee.
Marsh	William	First inspector of nuisances and medical inspector.
Mason	James C	b 1854. Schoolmaster.
Matcham	Charles	Last licensee of Catherine Wheel. Town surveyor in 1838.
Maud	John Lawes	1774-1839. Corporation member 1805-1835.
McLoughlin	William Charles	Mayor 1903 and 1923. Honorary treasurer of Colportage association. Lived in Portland House.

McOwan	W	Soup and coal fund.
Menefy	Henry	Director and shareholder in gas company. Actuary of Savings Bank. Lighting and pavement commissioner.
Millard	Theophilus	Subscriber to the Institute. Lighting and pavement commissioner.
Miller	Arthur James	Appointed curate in 1844.
Miller	James	b 1841. Nurseryman of Bridge Street.
Miller	William F	b 1835. Innkeeper.
Miller	Revd. W G	Debating society committee.
Mintram	George	b 1840. Policeman.
Moore	Henry Pratt	1836-1896. Coachbuilder. Alderman 1880-1898. Mayor 1878 and 1889. Choral society committee. Supporter of the cottage hospital. Director of Andover Penny Bank.
Moore	John P	d 1894. Mayor 1882. Director of Andover Waterworks Ltd. Councillor 1880-1883.
Moore	Robert H	Choral society committee.
Moore	William M	b 1827. Licensee of Railway Inn.
Moorehouse	R K	Manager of gas works. Debating society committee.
Moreton	John S	b 1845. Councillor.
Morrant	John G	b 1849. Tenant of Town Mill.
Mortimore	Thomas Heard	1804-1883. Tanner. Magistrate. Mayor 1857 and 1867. Director and shareholder of gas company. Supporter of cottage hospital. Soup and coal fund. Councillor 1835.
Mountford	William	Director of gas company.
Mundy	William	Member of corporation 1776-1801.
Mundy	Charles	Farmer. Council member 1835.
Mundy	Frank	b 1817. Licensee of New Inn.
Mundy	Hugh	1766-1821. Member of corporation 1804-1820. Council member 1835. Soup and coal fund.
Musselwhite	Herbert	1847-1888. Master of the workhouse. Died of typhoid fever.
Musson	William S	b 1840. Farmer at Picket Piece.
Neale	Thomas	Licensee of Catherine Wheel 1816-1818.
Neale	Ann	Licensee of the Catherine Wheel 1819-1823. Wife of Thomas.

Neale	George	b 1854. Andover Down farm
Neale	William	1758-1823. Member of corporation 1798-1821.
Ncpcan	Revd. E Y	Vicar of Appleshaw. Supporter of cottage hospital.
Newton	A J	Builder. Councillor.
Nicholls	Robert	b 1851. Draper.
Noyce	F R	Mayor 1912.
Nutley	William	Councillor 1891-1894.
Oram	George Ellis	b 1840. Brewer.
Oram	James	Shareholder in gas company.
Orchard	Henry	b 1853. Schoolmaster of the national school.
Packer	Samuel	b 1833. Tailor. Debating society committee.
Page	Thomas	Debating society committee. Councillor 1890-1893. Stonemason.
Paget	William	Andover MP 1841-1847.
Pain	Charles	Supporter of the cottage hospital.
Painter	Benjamin	Member of corporation 1811-1814.
Parker	Peter	1733-1809. Member of corporation 1802-1809.
Parker	Thomas H	Corporation member 1833-1835.
Parnell	Edward	b 1824. Licensee of Folly Inn.
Parsons	William	b 1816. Draper. Member of the Loyal Lion and Oak Lodge of Oddfellows. Murdered on 23rd November 1858. Assassin unknown.
Parsons	William Henry	1844-1911. Draper, Parsons & Hart. Choral society committee. Shareholder and director of Andover Waterworks. Chairman of Urban Sanitary Authority.
Payne	George S	Mayor 1848.
Pearse	Frederick	b 1846. Photographer.
Pedder	William	Headmaster of the grammar school 1798-1809.
Penton	Harvey	b 1845. River keeper.
Pern	F	Subscriber to Institute. Choral society committee. First secretary of cottage hospital.
Pettiford	Joseph	Master of the pest house.

Phillips	C J	Mayor 1897 and 1900. Vice president of debating society. Institute secretary.
Phillips	John	b 1815. Baker.
Phillips	Thomas	Mayor 1838 and 1846. Member of corporation 1833-1835.
Pike	William V	Institute secretary.
Piper	Robert	b 1812. Knife and scissor grinder.
Pitman	G W	First secretary of debating society.
Pitman	Henry	Corporation member 1828-1833.
Pitman	William I	Director of Andover Savings Bank. Member of corporation 1807-1835.
Pitman	William II	b 1798. Corporation member 1819-1828.
Pollen	Sir John Walter	1784-1863. of Redenham. Trustee of Andover Savings Bank. Andover MP 1820-1831, 1835-7.
Pool	William	Shareholder in gas company.
Pond	B B	Mayor 1902 and 1911. Vice president of debating society.
Ponting	Philip	1843-1908. Baker. Mayor 1898. Guardian of the poor. Shareholder in gas company and Catherine Wheel. Debating society committee. Member of the colportage society.
Poore	Dr. George Vivian	1843-1904. Supporter of the cottage hospital. Promoter of dry earth closets.
Poore	John	b 4th April 1809. Wine merchant. Mayor 1836, 1849 and 1860. Director of Andover Savings Bank. Lighting and pavement commissioner. Member of corporation 1822-1835. Council member 1835-1838.
Poore	Philip Henry	b 1834. Brewer and mineral water manufacturer. Superintendent of fire brigade.
Pope	James	b 1829. Licensee of Rose and Chequers.
Preedy	John	b 1814. Builder. Inspector of nuisances.
Proctor	George Alan	b 1832. Vicar of Hatherden.
Proctor	James S	On hospital committee. Director of Andover Penny Bank. Manager of waterworks.
Pugh	Edward	1743-1819. Member of corporation.

Putz	Miss H	Matron of cottage hospital 1897-1925.
Pyle	Walter	1745-1804. Grocer, Member of corporation 1769-1804. Bailiff on many occasions.
Randolph	Revd. Edward	Shareholder in Catherine Wheel.
Ransom	William	b 1807. Silk weaver.
Rashleigh	George Cumming	Vicar 1830-1835.
Reding	William	1774-1832. Member of corporation 1801-1831.
Reeks	Alfred	b 1840. Licensee of White Hart. Assistant curator of museum. Choral society committee. Councillor 1879-1888.
Reeks	J C	Mayor 1906 and 1910.
Reeves	John	Shareholder in gas company.
Reynard	Alfred W	Headmaster of the grammar school 1840-1843.
Reynolds	Edward	1836-1897. Mayor 1879. Director of Andover Penny Bank. Alderman 1883-1895. Lighting and pavement commissioner.
Reynolds	George K	b 1851. Estate agent and auctioneer. Bankrupt in 1887.
Reynolds	M E	Director of Andover Savings Bank.
Richards	Revd. Henry Manning	Curate. Subscriber to the Institute. Director of Andover Savings Bank. Soup and coal fund.
Ridding	Revd. Chas Henry	Vicar 1835-1869. Subscriber to the Institute
Roberts	Robert	b 1840. Licensee of Thompson's Arms Inn.
Rogers	F W	d 1898. Institute committee.
Satchel	John P	b 1844. Solicitor's managing clerk.
Scott	Frederick A	Institute committee.
Seton	G	Manager of gas works.
Shaw	Samuel	b 1812. Grocer. Clerk and then secretary of gas works. First secretary of Institute. Councillor in 1835.
Shaw	Francis Samuel	1849-1913. Son of Samuel above. Grocer. Shareholder and director of gas company. Guardian of the poor. Council member 1879-1882.

Sheppard	J K	Hospital committee.
Sherwood	Henry	1860-1917. Mayor 1895 and 1901. Councillor 1891-1895.
Sherwood	John	JP
Shubrick	Gen. Richard	Donated the clock for the toll house on Western Hill. Later transferred to Institute building.
Simcock	William	Chemist. Member of the jury which enquired into the death of William Parsons who was murdered in 1858.
Smallbone	James	b 1821. Licensee of Pelican Inn. Hired horses.
Smith	Charles Henry	b 1844. Watchmaker.
Smith	John W	Solicitor. Institute trustee who sold the Institute to the council in 1897. Shareholder in the gas company. Subscriber to the Institute. Supporter of the cottage hospital.
Smith	Joseph	Corporation member 1783-1802.
Smith	R H	Headmaster of the grammar school 1838-1840.
Smith	Thomas Assheton	1752-1828. Trustee of Andover Savings Bank. MP 1797-1821.
Smith	Thomas Assheton, jr.	1776-1856. MP 1821-1831.
Snary	Isaac	Conductor of choral society after W Bennett.
Snelgar	Edwin	b 1823. Coal merchant. Soup and coal fund.
South	Aaron	b 1840. Primitive Methodist minister.
Spinney	Edward	b 1841. Blacksmith in Charlton.
Spreadbury	Francis	b 1839. Editor of Andover Advertiser.
Stagg	George Hayter	1844-1896. County surveyor. Director of Catherine Wheel Coffee House. Choral society committee. Councillor 1880-1883.
Stears	William Morley	Constructed the gas works in 1838.
Stephens	Edmond R P	b 1846. Solicitor's clerk.
Stock	H	Treasurer of Andover Penny Bank.
Stockham	Sophia	b 1853. Headmistress at Charlton School.
Stockley	William	b 1842. Licensee of Jockey Inn.
Stout	Charles	Blacksmith. Caretaker of Institute. Shareholder in Catherine Wheel Coffee House.

Stride	Herbert	b 1827. Coach builder. Subscriber to the Institute.
Symons	James	Director and shareholder in the gas company. Director of Andover Savings Bank. Soup and coal fund. Member of the jury which enquired into the death of William Parsons who was murdered in 1858.
Tarrant	James	b 1805. Debating society committee.
Tarrant	Thomas	Shareholder in Catherine Wheel Coffee House.
Tasker	Robert	Subscriber to the Institute. Founder of the Waterloo Ironworks.
Tasker	William (senior)	Subscriber to the Institute. Founder of the Waterloo Ironworks.
Tasker	William (junior)	Subscriber to the Institute.
Taylor	A C	Soup and coal fund.
Temblett	Stephen	Manager of gas works 1889-1924.
Temblett	Garnet T	Managing director of gas works in 1937.
Thomas	A H	First secretary of Andover Penny Bank in 1875.
Thomas	Philip	b 1860. Manager of gas works.
Thomas	William Wells	Gas works clerk and shareholder.
Thompson	George II	Rector of Kimpton. Director of Andover Savings Bank. Member of corporation 1809-1829.
Thompson	Henry	1807-1866. JP. Mayor 1843, 1852 and 1861. Director of gas works. Trustee of the Institute. Choral society committee. Supporter of the cottage hospital. Soup and coal fund.
Thorpe	Richard	Auditor of the Catherine Wheel Coffee House Ltd.
Thresher	J H	Soup and coal fund.
Tilbury	John	b 1835. Councillor 1884-1893.
Titheridge	Maria	b 1838. Renowned soprano in St Mary's choir.
Todd	John Henry	1765-1834. Director of Andover Savings Bank. Member of the corporation 1805-1833. Postmaster of Andover in 1804,
Tredgold	Charles	1836-1899. Postmaster of Andover 1875-1898. Died at Ilfracombe.

Tredgold	H	Son of Charles. Postmaster at Andover 1898-1913.
Trinder	George	1825-1892. Upholsterer. Councillor 1884-1887.
Tubb	John	b 1835. Licensee of Queen Charlotte Inn.
Tull	William	b 1820. Baker. Debating society committee. On jury to enquire into the death of William Parsons who was murdered in 1858.
Turk	John	b 1856. Licensee of Hare and Hounds, Hatherden.
Turner	Joseph	Bricklayer who worked on the rebuilding of the Guildhall in 1825.
Turner	William	Mayor 1907.
Victor	Henry Husted	Appointed curate in 1837.
Wager	William	Licensee of Catherine Wheel 1808-1810.
Wakefield	James	Institute committee.
Wakeford	Joseph	Mayor 1841. Corporation member 1830-1835. Council member in 1835.
Walbey	Robert D	b 1815. Farmer. Soup and coal fund
Walmsley	William	1793-1829. Director of Andover Savings Bank. Corporation member 1822-1826.
Ward	P	Soup and coal fund
Wear	W F	Collector of district rates.
Webb	Thomas	Mayor 1904, 1908, 1909, 1918, 1919 and 1924. Debating society committee.
Webb	W W	Cottage hospital committee.
Wellesley	Henry	1846-1900. Andover MP 1874-1880; 3rd Duke of Wellington, 1884.
Wells	Longden	b 1851. Solicitor.
West	J	Director of Andover Savings Bank.
Westbury	Giles H	Mayor 1853. Subscriber to the Institute. Choral society committee, Gave endowment of £100 to cottage hospital.
White	Albert Henry	Mayor 1893.
White	Francis Henry	Appointed curate 1847.
White	George Turner	1854-1899. Station master.
White	George D	b 1856. Policeman.
White	Revd. H M	First president of choral society.
Wickham	George	Corporation member 1833-1835.

Wignell	William	Licensee of Catherine Wheel 1811-1815.
Wildey	John	Corporation member 1813-1820. Bailiff 1831-1832.
Williams-Freeman	Dr. J P	Hospital committee; local archaeologist.
Wilson	Richard	Subscriber to the Institute.
Wiltshire	Benjamin	Shareholder in gas company.
Wimshurst	Henry	Manager of gas works 1875-1879.
Windover	John	Roofing contractor. Roofed the Guildhall in 1825.
Winter	Henry	b 1825. Mail cart driver.
Withers	William	Councillor. Lighting and pavement commissioner.
Witton	Revd. James Cecil	1850-1905. Headmaster of grammar school 1880-1905. Debating society.
Witts	David	b 1837. Scavenger.
Wolfe	E	Supporter of cottage hospital.
Wood	Charles	Subscriber to the Institute. Supporter of the cottage hospital. Lighting and pavement commissioner.
Woods	John Thomas	b 1840. Farmer. Mayor 1884. Committed suicide.
Worgan	Benjamin	Member of corporation 1771-1805.
Young	George	Provision dealer. Cottage hospital committee. On jury to enquire into the death of Williams Parsons who was murdered in 1858.
Zincke	Foster Barham	Appointed curate in 1840.

INDEX TO THE FOUR ARTICLES